Rave Reviews for *30 Days to Better Flycasting*

"We can't think of anyone within the flyfishing community who has more passion, energy and enthusiasm for teaching flycasting than Berris Samples. His text takes the reader through the basic ABCs of flycasting and beyond, touching base on each and every detail. This book should be in the hands of anyone attempting to learn flycasting."

— Barry & Cathy Beck, international flyfishing photographers, tour hosts and seminar leaders (based in Benton, Pa.) and co-authors of *Fly-Fishing the Flats*

"Berris was one of the first Americans who flyfished in our river Deutsche Traun. I have known him for over 10 years, and he is truly a great flyfisher. I am sure that this innovative book of his will make you a better flycaster or casting instructor."

— Rudi Heger, owner of Traun River Products, Bavaria, Germany

"Fellow FFFer Berris Samples has hit a home run with this great book.... After a combined total of more than 50 years experience in fly tying and flyfishing, we thought we had seen it all regarding flycasting books and videos. We were wrong! This great book approaches the subject from the instructor/student perspective, explaining casting problems and their solutions in an easy-to-understand format. This book is a must-have for any flycasting instructor."

— Al & Gretchen Beatty, owners of BT's Fly Fishing Products in Delta, Colo., and co-authors of three books, including the *FFF Fly Pattern Encyclopedia*

"Bear is the most complete flyfisher I have ever known. He has fished all over the world, mastering every nuance of the sport. In *30 Days to Better Flycasting*, he combines humor, compelling examples, and clear, concise instructions to create a book that can help every flyfisher — beginner and expert alike — become a better caster. This work sets the standard by which all other casting guides will be measured."

— Norm Zeigler, Sanibel, Florida-based travel/outdoor writer for the European edition of *The Stars and Stripes*, and author of the upcoming book *Irati Evenings, Dunajec Days: A Flyfisher's European Journal*

"A new, fresh and welcomed approach to learning and teaching flycasting. Bear's new book will improve your flycasting whether you are a beginner or a seasoned caster."

— Bob Jacklin, member of the FFF Fly Casting Certification Board of Governors and owner of Jacklin's Fly Shop in West Yellowstone, Montana

30 days to better flycasting

Your guide to mastering the art of flycasting

By Berris "Bear" Samples

Foreword by Randi Swisher
Illustrations by Mike Stidham
Photography by Collin Turner

Publisher:
 Bryan Brandenburg
 AmazingOutdoors.com
 965 E. Murray Holladay Road, Suite 1A,
 Salt Lake City, UT 84117
 (801) 858-3450
 www.AmazingOutdoors.com

Author:
 Berris "Bear" Samples

Editor:
 Marcia C. Dibble,
  AmazingOutdoors.com

Illustrator:
 Mike Stidham

Cover design:
 Cory Maylett,
  AmazingOutdoors.com

Photographer:
 Collin Turner,
  AmazingOutdoors.com

Contributing photographers:
 Bear Samples
 Greg Connor
 Jimmy Chang
 Todd Hood (cover photo of
  Geoff Samples and
  Chanika McLelland)
 Del Dykes, Reel Action
  (cover photo of mahimahi)

Printer:
 Bertelsmann Services Inc.
 Valencia, California

©2000 AmazingOutdoors.com

Printed in the USA.

All rights reserved. No part of this book may be reproduced in any form or by any means without permission in writing from the publisher, AmazingOutdoors.com, 965 E. Murray Holladay Road, Suite 1A, Salt Lake City, UT 84117.

Library of Congress Catalog Card Number: 00-192953
ISBN: 0-9671738-7-6

Dedication

This book is dedicated to Brenda, Geoff and Ty, my "River Runs Through It" family, who have allowed their minister husband and father to play and cast with them in waters around the world.

Acknowledgments

Many thanks are due to all of those who team together to make a book possible. I have been fortunate and blessed to be surrounded by talented and inspiring people. A special thanks to Randi Swisher, who has provided an outstanding example of skilled casting, trusted me to be part of the Sage casting team, and was instrumental in developing and evaluating Bear's Casting Aid.

Appreciation goes to the modern "greats" of our flycasting sport, including Joan Wulff, Mel Krieger, Lefty Kreh, Doug Swisher, Bob Jacklin, Gary Borger, Steve Rajeff and Bruce Richards. I've learned a great deal from their articles, books, videos and seminars. I only hope to contribute a small piece to their base of knowledge.

Mike Stidham has honored this book as he has so many others with his special art. He has a wonderful way of getting to the heart and soul of flyfishing on canvas, and I'm always awed to see how he creates and captures the essence of the sport.

My friends at *Utah Outdoors* magazine, Bryan Brandenburg, Dave Webb, Sam Webb, Jennifer Czekai and their photography, layout, marketing, editing and production staff, all contributed to the final product. This innovative company has created the web host site, AmazingOutdoors.com, which places an outdoors encyclopedia at our fingertips.

Recognition goes to our flyfishing conservation and education organizations, the Federation of Fly Fishers (FFF) and Trout Unlimited (TU), who tirelessly promote flycasting education in their publications and seminars. The flyfishing world owes a debt of gratitude to the FFF for establishing the Fly Casting Instructor's Certification Program. Without question, the international quality of instruction has improved through this structured program.

Thank you to the flyfishing industry companies that have supported this work and countless other flyfishing education projects — Sage Rod Company, Tibor Fly Reels, Simms, Scientific Anglers and Ex Officio.

A final thanks to my many flyfishing friends around the globe, who are too numerous to name. Your fellowship and camaraderie have enriched my life and joy in living.

Forecast: Table of Contents

DEDICATION 5

ACKNOWLEDGMENTS 6

FOREWORD 9

INTRODUCTION 11

PART ONE: PROLEGOMENON 17
    A. Bear's Casting Aid 19
    B. Flycasting Ability Levels 23
    C. Teaching Youth to Cast 28
    D. Women and Fly Rods 33
    E. Flycasting for Seniors 37
    E. Shaping Up 42

PART TWO: BEGINNER 45
    A. The Proper Grip 47
    B. Poetry in Motion:
        Using the Correct Body Position 51
    C. Casting's No. 1 Problem: The Floppy Wrist 55
    D. Getting the Slack Out 58

PART THREE: INTERMEDIATE 61
    A. Roll Casting for Results 63
    B. Troubled Loops 68
    C. The Infamous Tailing Loop 72
    D. Learning to Shoot 75
    E. Going for Distance 79

PART FOUR: ADVANCED 83
    A. Casting Problems with Sinking Lines 85
    B. On Time, On Target: Flycasting Accuracy 89
    C. Hauling for Optimum Line Speed 94
    D. Beating Windy Situations 99

PART FIVE: EXPERT 103
    A. Presentation Casts 105
    B. Saltwater Mastery 110
    C. Becoming a Certified Casting Instructor 116
    D. Sharpening the Mental Game of Flycasting 120

CLOSE: LAST CAST 125

SUGGESTED READING AND VIEWING 127

INDEX 129

AMAZINGOUTDOORS.COM RESOURCES 131

AUTHOR'S BIOGRAPHY 132

Foreword

My first contact with Berris Samples was about 10 years ago at the Federation of Fly Flyfishers Conclave. Berris was teaching the Youth Conclave in West Yellowstone, Montana, and asked me to assist him with the flycasting instruction. I was quickly impressed not only with his ability to teach the youngsters the basics of flycasting, but also with his unique style of breaking down the casting mechanics into a vocabulary that these future flyfishers could relate to and understand. Through his commitment to the FFF, Berris became a Master Certified Instructor and has since contributed his time and expertise to teaching thousands of people.

Being an Army Chaplain for the U.S. Army, Berris taught flycasting to ranking officers as well as soldiers in the field. I remember when Berris sent me a photo from Desert Storm, on the border of Iraq and Iran, showing a squadron of soldiers practicing their casting on the sands of the desert next to Army tanks.

Berris has had the opportunity to fish all over the world. His in-depth flyfishing knowledge, for all species of fish, as well as quality instruction in tackle and strategy concepts provide further enhancement to his students. This experience coupled with his high energy and positive attitude make him a standout instructor.

This book is a quick and easy manual that provides detailed, to-the-point methods to make you a better caster. For many years now, flycasting instruction has become a "big word," complicated process, wherein instructors teach that their way is the only way. Unfortunately, many instructors don't realize there are myriad styles of casting and multiple ways to accomplish teaching the basic principles. The proper method of correcting mistakes in casting is instrumental in enhancing anyone's casting. Berris has done a great service in providing concise, easy to understand concepts that all flycasters can use.

Randi Swisher,
Bainbridge Island, Washington

INTRODUCTION

Why learn flycasting? The number one skill at the heart of flyfishing is flycasting. Reading the water, presentation and fly selection are all critical skills, but without the necessary cast, you have weakened your ability to take fish. Ask any flyfishing guide, fresh or saltwater, and they will tell you that they wish their clients were better casters.

More than 5 million people in America claim flyfishing as one of their primary sports and pastimes. (I know it often seems as if they have all arrived on our home water for our favorite hatch!) One thing that each of these fishers shares in common is that they are all flycasters. Another thing all of these folks share is that they all blow casts and make casting mistakes. From the pros to the rank beginners making their first casts, everyone makes mistakes. Reaching that distant fish that is five feet beyond your best cast can be the height of frustration. Why can't that $200 (or more) piece of high-tech graphite propel your line to the prized target?

The purpose of *30 Days to Better Flycasting* is to make you a better caster, and thus, help you catch more fish. Also, improving your casting gives you greater pleasure and self-satisfaction in flyfishing. Just as most people measure their fishing skills by the number of fish landed, flycasting skills can be developed to show improvement. My approach to casting is to locate the problems in anyone's cast and to teach the proper method of correction. This style is in contrast to many books and clinics that simply teach various casts. I want you to "undo" and "unlearn" the bad habits that keep you from being a truly good caster. Flawless casting means just that.

The starting place for good casting is desire. Do you really want to be a better flycaster, and are you willing to work to improve? I see countless people spending hundreds of dollars on ski, golf and tennis lessons and camps, while these same people pick up a fly rod and expect to be a natural born expert. It just doesn't happen. In contrast to other sports, people rarely practice flycasting. Golfers will go to the driving range and hit bucket after bucket of balls; tennis players will practice serving for an hour. Where are our flyfishers? I rarely see flyfishers practice their casting.

It is almost impossible to fix your casting mistakes or bad habits while you are fishing. Our focus on the stream is on catching, not casting. But I've found it to be like salt in a wound when someone is outcasting me at the river and catching more fish. You must determine to get better and improve

About 20 years ago, I was fishing for large brown trout at a lake in Wisconsin. As bad luck would have it, these cruising fish were just beyond my range. I literally tried for hours to reach those fish. To try to achieve distance, I would wade deep in my chest waders, then stand on tiptoe to get a better backcast. Moving rocks off shore, I tried to form a casting platform. Just two more feet of line and I could reach their cruising area. As good luck would have it, one of these steroid monsters finally struck my fly. It launched into the air like a cruise missile. My mind's eye still pictures that fish at dusk with water being thrown in all directions and the sound of a car wreck as the fish crashed down. The fish broke off as it charged for the bottom. Shocked, I reeled in and quit. Jaded from all of my failed casting, I was men-

Brad Connor holds a trophy brown, the type of payoff you can expect with better casting.

tally exhausted when the fish finally struck.

We all have stories about lost fish or unobtainable ones. How many of these were related to poor casting ability? *Good flycasting means catching more and better fish.* You might want to argue my maxim, but all of our flyfishing professionals are standing in my court. Good flycasting means better presentation, longer distance, overcoming wind or other challenging conditions, and keeping your fly on the water with fewer false casts.

It is my goal to teach you to be a better caster. Personally, I determined that I was going to be an expert. If I was going to spend a small fortune each year on equipment and excursions, I thought I had best improve on my weakest area. After many years of effort, I am now a Master Certified Instructor and cast for Sage Rod Company. Each year I teach hundreds of people flycasting, and both of my sons have won casting tournaments around the U.S.

You will need to help me if you are going to advance and improve. First, use the very best equipment that you can afford. You might laugh, but I know people who drive beater cars just so they have the cash for top fly gear. Go to a fly shop and ask for assistance. Your reel is not critical, but purchase an excellent fly rod and weight-forward floating line. If you settle for a $15 line, you will end up making $15 casts.

Next, get ahold of current casting books and videos by other flyfishing professionals. Joan Wulff, Mel Kreiger, Lefty Kreh, Gary Borger and Doug Swisher have all done books and videos. Fill your head with casting knowledge and wisdom. Learn the terminology. Practice their techniques.

When you have the opportunity, take a casting lesson. Here is a tip: Never buy a fly rod from a shop without them giving you a free lesson. That is just adding value to their sale. If they can't give you a good lesson from a certified instructor, then ask for your money back. You can also take lessons at fishing shows and conclaves.

Your regular assignments in this book are to go outside in a nonfishing setting and **practice your casting**. Practice on water, in the yard, at a park, or in a parking lot. Pavement can be a bit hard on lines, but practice is more important than wear and tear. Make sure you have plenty of casting room and aren't going to hook any 18-wheelers on your fore- or backcasts. My son, Geoff, blew up a 2-weight rod on a '92 Plymouth van. I know cars to beat rods every time.

This book's flexible glue binding makes it easy to press the book open at a casting area you want to work on and place it open on a chair or stool for easy reference while practicing. Read the practice directions closely. You may want to invite a friend to practice with you so you can evaluate each other's form.

Also, don't forget that you can **practice in pantomime fashion without a rod**. I learned to cast a tight, narrow loop by practicing in my car while driving! And actually, I wasn't as crazy as some cell phone users: I would at least stop at a light before going into a double-haul. Maybe you'll turn as many heads as I have.

To assist your casting and tighten your loops, Bear's Casting Aid is available separately and packaged with this book. Read the section on using the Aid and practice with it. Don't be embarrassed to use it while fishing. Many fishers are wearing it on the stream and not worrying about hinging their wrists. If you need additional Casting Aids for yourself or friends, you can find them at your local fly shop or they can be ordered direct from AmazingOutdoors.com.

30 Days to Better Flycasting is truly meant to help you improve your skills within 30 days! If you will dedicate 30 days to this regimen of lessons, practice and study, you cannot help but benefit. *Any* casters can vastly enhance their proficiency in 30 days.

In one summer I have witnessed a total novice who had never picked up a fly rod skyrocket to casting as an advanced intermediate. Working with prospective certified flycasting instructors, it takes approximately four weeks of focused preparation to prepare for exam testing. From beginner to expert, every caster could use this season of committed workouts.

In this book, I will describe flycasting mistakes that we all make at times. Closely examine the photos to visually pick up on the problem. Then, follow the suggested steps to correct your miscues. Stick with me. We'll work on your casting to groove your stroke, smooth your power and tighten your loops. Before you know it, your casting will be better than ever with more fish to show for it. By working through the book, you should advance at least one skill level in your casting ability.

Also, learn to enjoy casting for casting's sake. Get into the rhythm and flow and timing. You'll find yourself closer in harmony with yourself and the stream.

Part One: Prolegomenon

Prolegomenon is a Greek word that I learned during my ministerial studies that means "first words" or "first things." It is related to our English word "prologue." In beginning our excursion into flycasting, I want to state my biases and avoid some assumptions, as well as show the uniqueness of this flycasting book and hopefully how it can help people with their casting.

The book's design

First off, about this large typeface. Because the special flexible binding of this book is designed to enable you to set the book open-faced on a chair while practicing in the yard or in a park, we used large type to allow you to easily read the book without having to bend down and lose the casting form you are attempting to master. Don't hesitate to press the book open; the glue was created to readily bounce back.

To further enable you to use this book while practicing, many of the key ideas, forms etc. (such as the **"V" grip** or **"S" cast**) are marked here by boldface type to make them stand out.

Our terminology

Mel Krieger has graced flycasting with his artful style and superb instructional technique — he will always be known for his "down/up" direction in double hauling. I also follow his written usage of the terms "flyfishing," "flyfisher" and "flycasting." I find flyfishing and flycasting to be sports unto themselves and not just methods or approaches to fishing. Flyfishing, flyfisher and flycasting all capture the passion of placing a fly upon the water. As lovers of flyfishing, I hope we can all appreciate the philology of these words and my use of them.

Bear's Casting Aid

Over the years, I've worked with hundreds of people on their flycasting with good results. To help with the casting stroke, I have had people stick the rod butt underneath a long-sleeve shirt or use their opposite (line) hand to lock the rod butt against the wrist on the casting arm. These methods are somewhat adequate, yet an actual product was needed.

I knew what I wanted to devise: It had to be simple, user-friendly, inexpensive — and to really work. First and foremost, my casting aid had to make a flyfisher a better caster.

After trial and error with various materials, my flexible nylon strap system — Bear's Casting Aid — was developed.

Since hinging, flexing or bending the wrist is the No. 1 problem in flycasting, my Casting Aid is the solution. Use it in all of your casting practice. The rod butt slides into the fabric tube sleeve, which holds the rod in the correct position, then the strap Velcros over your wrist. Adjust the size to fit comfortably — don't

A student uses the Casting Aid during a lesson with Bear.

overtighten and create unnecessary pressure. After you've put on the Aid, you'll find that your hand fits lower down on the rod grip. This will also help you develop good form for distance casting.

This is the first time that a casting-assistance device has been offered with a casting book. Together, these tools should help you along the path to much-improved flycasting.

Practicing with the Aid

Let me describe using the Casting Aid for the pick-up and lay-down cast and for false casting.

To begin the pick-up and lay-down cast, make sure your line is laid out several feet straight to the front and your rod tip is held no more than six inches above the grass or water. Lift the rod to an almost vertical position beside your face. The Aid will keep your wrist from falling too far to the rear. Power the rod to the front, aiming at about eye level. Lower the rod after your line extends to the front. You will feel the Casting Aid secure your wrist and keep it tight or locked. This is a little awkward-feeling, but the rod is bending properly and doing the work. The rod will track in a nearly straight line and help to tighten your loop size (make it smaller).

False casting is vastly improved when the Casting Aid is employed. Practice by starting with the same "line straight, rod tip low" position as above. Use a short stroke for a short cast of 25-30 feet. When stopping the rod to the front or rear, allow the line to unfurl until it forms a "J" or candy cane on its side. Power the rod in the opposite direction and link a sequence of three, back to front. Can you tell that the Aid rescued you? Because of your tight wrist, the rod cannot flop to the rear in a large arc. You should have more power and energy in your cast than ever before. Also, the line energy is directed more in a straight line to the front and rear, which allows for shooting line and distance.

Demonstrating how the rod butt slides into Bear's Casting Aid.

Utilizing the Aid on stream

Can you use Bear's Casting Aid in fishing situations? Absolutely! Our testing proved that the Aid was very effective for better casting on stream. And because of its simple black color, it doesn't stand out like a road sign saying "Warning: Poor caster ahead."

From a practical perspective, we all want to improve our casting and catch more fish. The Casting Aid helps you focus on your fishing and not worry about the casting as much.

After practicing awhile with the Aid, put it down and you'll find that the casts you have worked on come naturally. Get out the Aid on those days when a wind could give you trouble: A tighter loop is more effective in those conditions than an open one. Once you find that your wrist is not hinging and that you are getting the proper feel, the Casting Aid can be set aside until you want to use it for tune-ups, or you can share it with a friend. Beginners and intermediates should use Bear's Casting Aid until they gain control of their casting loops.

After spending several hundred dollars on a first-rate fly rod, you'll be happy to have Bear's Casting Aid bring out that rod's best qualities.

If your friends or family want to join you for casting practice, you can order Bear's Casting Aid directly from Amazing Outdoors.com, or you'll find it at your local fly shop. For the price of a few flies and the fraction of the cost of a casting lesson, the Aid will get everyone into better flycasting.

Bear demonstrates using the Aid while casting on the Provo River.

Flycasting Ability Levels

Believe it or not, there is no national, or international for that matter, standard for charting flycasting ability levels. If you take a lesson at a shop or from a casting professional, you may receive evaluations like, "You're pretty good, just keep working on tighter loops," or "Keep casting like that and you are going to catch a lot more fish," or better still, "My 80-year-old grandmother could outcast you with tubular fiberglass!"

But just how good — or bad — are you? Are you progressing with your flycasting or stuck at a level? Skiing clearly illustrates where the sport of flyfishing should head. If you were an alpine skier, you could take an evaluation lesson that would place you at a certain ability and skill level. Either on your own or with additional lessons, you could then seek to advance to more difficult terrain and end up at level 9 or double black diamond ability.

Currently, the Federation of Fly Fishers is overseeing the international flycasting instructor certification program. In less than 10 years, the FFF has standardized certification and produced the best instructors available. To become a basic or master certified instructor, you must possess advanced knowledge, casting skills and instructional ability. Why not use some of the FFF standards to delineate flycasting ability levels?

Creating measurable standards

I suggest creating an ability level standard that would be in print and also used by instructors so that flyfishers could determine how they might improve and advance in the sport. There are four general levels used today: beginner, intermediate, advanced and expert. By establishing an accepted standard, flycasters could be insured that as they take lessons and work to improve they could know which ability level they have reached. Flycasting ability levels should state what skills are necessary before advancing to a higher plane. I'll list the major items that I believe are required at each level.

Beginner skills

Beginners are usually those who have just picked up a fly rod or who don't spend much time in the sport. If you are a casual flyfisher, it is pretty difficult to find much improvement in your game. I believe a beginner must master the basics of casting. They should be able to perform a pick-up and lay-down cast at 25-30 feet. Beginning casters should make elementary false casts with medium to wide loops. Roll casts are fairly easy to master, so a novice must work at a standard cast of 20 to 25 feet. In all basic casting, the line should lie straight at the end of a cast. Just think, if you can cast pretty well at 25-30 feet, a good deal of your casting situations are covered.

Intermediates

The intermediate level is where the majority of our typical flyfishers get stuck. The major problem to overcome at this ability level is bending or hinging your wrist. If you do not learn to stiffen or lock the movement of your wrist, the rod arcs over to the front and rear and leaves the line powerless. You'll also continue to form medium to wide loops. Intermediates must master the power stroke move so that the rod is speeded up to a definite stop. This forces the rod tip into a tight, narrow arc, which produces good line speed and narrow loops.

By reaching this level, an intermediate caster should distance cast to 50-60 feet. By maintaining a good loop in false casting and shooting line, this is a very manageable distance. Again, shooting line is a critical skill for this level. Accuracy is needed up to 40 feet, and you should be close to targets up to this range. Backhand or opposite-shoulder casting is also required, which is a big help under windy conditions. The roll cast must now be powered to 30-35 feet.

As you can tell, it's not easy to progress beyond this ability level. More than three-fourths of our flycasters are at the intermediate level or below. One very practical reason for this is that with intermediate skills you'll be able to cover most flyfishing situations, so most flyfishers do not see a significant reason to

30 Days to Better Flycasting **PROLEGOMENON** | 25

Bear discusses good body mechanics with a mixed group of novices.

improve. But with good instruction, working out your bad habits, and using good equipment, you can move up the skill ladder.

The advanced level

There aren't a lot of advanced flycasters showcasing their skills on our lakes and rivers. It takes a dedicated commitment and practice to get there

Why would you even want to be advanced anyway? I've spent thousands of dollars on flyfishing trips around the world and I spend a small fortune on the best equipment that I can afford, so to gain the most from my investment I want to improve. When I'm fishing the flats on the Yucatan, I don't want to blow a cast on a trophy permit. Remember my adage, "Good casting means more and better fish." Finally, I find flyfishing to be an extremely challenging, lifetime sport. I want to be the best flycaster that I can make myself to be.

The FFF has set a standard for being an advanced caster by having a person pass the Basic Casting Instructor Certification Program. Whether a person takes the test is immaterial, but it contains an important skill set to master. An advanced caster usually has a good knowledge base about casting from reading, watching videos and instruction from the pros. Many advanced casters are flycasting instructors, guides and professionals.

What does it take to reach the advanced mark? With a standard floating fly line, can you cast 75 feet? The critical skill for advanced flycasters is learning to double haul with maximum casting efficiency. Other skills are roll casting with accuracy up to 45-50 feet. Because tailing loops will ruin any casting, you should know what causes them and how to correct them. Presentation casts and line control are also important, so add reach casts to right and left, pile casts and side arm casts to 40 feet.

Becoming an expert

The highest level of flycasting ability is expert. I estimate that experts make up less than five percent of people involved in the sport.

Maybe you've attended a flyfishing show where one of the professionals amazed the audience, or your guide for an outing had superhuman skills. There are very few "born" flycasters; most are made. Most expert casters have worked at casting for many years and honed their skills to second nature. When you see the experts perform, it all appears very easy for them because it has simply become like riding a bike. Experts may differ in style, but they have mastered the physics and mechanics of casting and there are very few flaws or errors in their methods. If you ever have the opportunity, don't miss a show from Joan Wulff, Mel Krieger, Lefty Kreh, Doug Swisher, Barry and Cathy Beck, Randi Swisher, Steve Rajeff or Gary Borger.

It is only logical that our most difficult casting settings and situations have produced our best casters. Saltwater and steelhead flyfishing demand long casts in windy settings. Inefficient casting on the flats or on a big river makes your trip a total waste. The indigenous guides of the Caribbean and Pacific have developed excellent skills from casting in 20-mile-per-hour winds day after day. Tight loops and driving, powerful casts are the norm.

Bear plies his expert skills on a winter stream.

Testing for expert skills is the requirement for a Master Certified Instructor with the FFF. An expert/master caster must reach out and touch 85 feet in distance casting. You must cast with accuracy to targets up to 55 feet in regular fashion and over the opposite shoulder. A roll cast must be accurate to 50 feet and be made with a shooting technique to 55. Controlling your casting loops while moving from vertical to horizontal with 40 feet of line means exact timing. Experts should be able to make more difficult presentation casts such as aerial mends, curve casts and "S" casts.

Becoming an expert caster is like being a golf or tennis pro. You have developed the skills to teach others and to enjoy all of the challenges that difficult flycasting situations can dish out.

Advancing on the skill ladder takes good instruction, practice, dedication and hard work. I've assisted many people to improve. Set your goals and standards high. All of your efforts will pay off big fishing dividends.

Teaching Youth to Cast

You might wonder, when should children begin flycasting? What type of equipment is needed? Are there any special tips or techniques that help kids learn faster?

I began flyfishing at age 13 with really awful equipment. It was the best that I could afford with my savings at the time, but it is amazing that I could even get the line out 20 feet. Today's outfits weigh half of what I tried to use. Current equipment allows youngsters to get started in flyfishing at an early age.

When I became a parent, flycasting at our house was much like eating or going to church. Both my boys started at age 5. They saw dad practicing in the yard, so as good imitators, they wanted to try as well. With supervision, they began making their first casts. Having instructed hundreds of youngsters now, I'd have to say the best age to begin is about 7.

The right equipment

The main problem for children is physical — they have small hands and little arm strength. To overcome these limitations, young children (ages 5 to 10) should use shorter, lighter rods. If you can provide a 5- or 6-foot rod in a 5- or 6-weight line, you have effectively reduced equipment weight.

When selecting a rod, it is very important to get one with a small grip to fit the hands of children. This would be about half the size as some adult rod handles. Another trick is to overline the rod by using one line weight heavier than recommended by the rod manufacturer. Doing this causes the rod to bend more deeply and load easier. Match this to a beginner's line of about 60 feet, little backing and a lightweight reel. I cringe when I discover young people using granddad's old outfit or mom's "used up" hand-me-down.

Have the youngest children practice their casting by using two hands to hold the rod. Don't worry about a proper thumb on top grip. You want children to have twice their arm strength by using two hands. Take your young protegees to the yard and begin by

Bear instructs a young student.

letting them wave about 10 feet of line around them in the air. They will learn by feel, and you want them to have some fun playing around.

Getting the cast right requires that you teach the basics and mechanics of good casting. Kids only need to learn two casts: the pick-up and lay-down cast, and the roll cast.

Teaching the basic cast

Let's start with a pick-up and lay-down, or basic cast. Always start with the line straight to the front and the rod tip low, i.e. within six inches of the ground or water. Don't just turn your young student loose, but hold the rod with them and perform the cast together. With 15 feet of line out, lift the rod smartly and stop beside the child's ear. After the line unfurls to the rear, power the rod to the front and lower the rod. After a few minutes, my boys would exclaim, "Dad, let me do it by myself!" If they seem to be getting it, let them make a few casts by themselves.

The key thing for adults to have when teaching youngsters is patience. Good casting takes a long time. Keep your practice sessions short, because kids are used to sound bites. I recommend 15 minutes. If your child is not with it that day, just put the rod away. I'm a firm believer that you should never apply too much force to big fish or little children.

I use three casting games with children that are fun to play and hold their interest. The first practice game is called yard fishing. The adult kneels about 20 feet in front of the child on an open lawn. You should rig the youth rod with a bright piece of yarn as a fly. The object of the game is for the young person to cast the fly to the adult, who is the "big trout." When the child casts within a short reach, the adult should grab the yarn fly and cry out "fish on!" or "you've got one!" Then allow the youngster to reel the fish in. Be sure to give the line some tugs to simulate the feel and play of a real fish.

The next game is for accuracy and could be called "catching dolls" or "catching Beanie Babies." Place several of these targets about the yard in a semi-circle at varying distances form 15 to 20 feet. See how close our beginning caster can get to their fun targets. Reward your youngster with M&Ms, Skittles or another small treat.

A final game is for older youth who need more of a yard challenge. We place a stuffed cotton fish on top of a remote-controlled car and fly the fish all over the yard! It's even a fun game for adults. As it turns out, we usually all fight over driving the car and make the fish perform some unusual stunts. Again, the object is to get your fly close to the fish.

The roll cast

Our second important cast for youth is the roll cast. A roll cast is a good choice to use when fishing creeks or in areas where trees or bushes wouldn't allow a backcast. It keeps the fly in the water and is easy to perform.

Using the same two-hand method as described earlier, practice the youth roll cast on water, such as a pond or slow-moving creek. Another trick is to spray water on a flat driveway or parking

Mel Krieger helps a youngster improve her casting form.

lot. If enough covers the surface, it will work like a 1/4-inch deep pond. Water is necessary to hold the line or anchor it during the stop of the cast. This tension causes the rod to load and make the forward cast. Begin like a regular cast with the line straight and rod tip low. With a 6-foot rod you will only need 15 feet of line out. Lift the rod and pull the line toward you, letting the rod cock slightly from the vertical to the rear. The line should loop toward the rear, with a portion lying on the water to the front. After stopping the rod and line, power the rod to the front like a normal cast. Don't rotate the rod toward the water, but drive it forward and lower it. The line will pile up in the front if you lower your rod too quickly — power it in an arc that moves down to the water.

Older youth ages 13 and above can begin using equipment that is close to an adult's. Most do best with a rod of about 8 feet with a 5- or 6-weight line. These young people should use typical one-hand casting since they have adequate arm strength. Bear's

Casting Aid is sized so that it can adjust to smaller wrists. Simply tighten the velcro strap a bit more. Teach adolescents the pick-up and lay-down cast and the roll cast, and add false casting. Play the same sorts of games as with the younger group. Have the older youth try to extend their casting to 30 feet and farther.

False casting

False casting is back and forth movement of the rod that extends the line to back and front while keeping the line in the air. It is used for accuracy, adding line and distance, changing direction of your cast and drying out a dry fly. To practice, work with 20-25 feet of line out with the line straight and rod tip low. Lift the rod and power the line to the rear. As the line forms a loop to the back and forms a "J" or candy cane lying on its side, bring the rod to the front with a power stroke. Reverse the procedure and perform a cast to the front with your timing signal being the "J." Aim the casts parallel to the ground in both directions. After making about three false casts in each direction, present your yarn fly to the front and allow it to fall. Pull off a longer length of line and see if you can cast it.

Many young people are just as good at casting as adults. Provide them with the proper equipment, instruction and encouragement and our youngsters are prepared for the stream. When you see the beaming smile of a child who has landed her first fish on a fly, you will know that all of your efforts in teaching a young person to cast are worth it.

Women and Fly Rods

It is exciting to see so many women picking up a fly rod to join the sport. Surveys have found flyfishing to be one of the fastest growing women's sports in America. It is understandable, because women are enjoying many other outdoor pursuits, and there is now a great deal of flyfishing equipment made just for women. Regularly, you will see casting clinics for "women only." I enjoy teaching women because they tend to be laid-back, enjoy casting as a sport unto itself, and don't overpower too much during practice.

Randi Swisher gives a private lesson at a Sage clinic.

The right equipment

Generally speaking, women should select 8- to 8 1/2- foot, 5-weight rods. When balanced with a light reel, even smaller women will not have trouble casting an entire day. Many rod companies are producing models specifically for women. When selecting a rod, try to find one that matches your casting ability. At a fly shop, I witnessed a woman comparing two different brands. Both rods had a moderate action, but she was much better with one than the other. Also, make sure to fit the rod grip to your hand. Once, a woman asked me how I liked her setup for an upcoming trip. As my mouth gaped open, she asked what my problem was. My observation was that the rod grip would fit Shaq O'Neill. She promptly returned the rod for another.

Preparing the body

One major problem that I see in women's casting is that many are not physically prepared. Arm strength is not critical, but if you cast an entire day on stream, use sinking lines, or employ heavier rods for salmon, steelhead or saltwater species, you need extra power. Weight machines or simple barbells can give you a boost, and you may want to try squeezing a tennis ball or one of the new hand strengtheners. It is surprising how much energy is transmitted through your rod hand during casting. My Casting Aid can also give you an extra confidence-building edge. Bear's Casting Aid sells just as well with women as men, and female flyfishers are usually not embarrassed to practice with the Aid or even fish with it.

Since women generally do not have the strength of men, they need to approach their casting just a little smarter. Work to become a pin-point-accurate caster. For more work and greater distances, use body motion to rock back and move forward with your cast. More than men, women should learn to shoot line and double

Karen Williams shows off a trophy at Monster Lake, in Wyoming.

Master caster Joan Wulff demonstrates good loops by hand casting with yarn.

haul. These critical line-speed techniques are a major help in a wind and for casting distance.

Monster Lake is one of the premier private fisheries in the West. Located near Cody, Wyo., this lake produces huge brook, cutthroat, brown and rainbow trout. On one outing there, Karen Williams, who began flyfishing at midlife, took a strategic position on a sandy point and cast dry flies all day. It was easy on her arm casting an 8-weight rod with a floating line. We teased her that the fishing would be like Alaska and to come prepared. As it turned out, she took 30 fish, the largest being a 7-pound brown. Over half of her total were over five pounds. At the end of the day, she looked whipped. I asked, "Did you get worn out on that 8-weight?" to which she slyly replied, "No, but I don't think I could play another fish." Touche!

Using the skills you already have

Some women refrain from casting a fly rod because they don't feel coordinated enough. But if you swing a tennis racket or golf club, you are well on your way. Any hand/eye-coordination sport translates easily into flycasting. Other women are hesitant to enter the traditional hunter domain of men. But as women give flyfishing a try, they usually enjoy the artistic flow of casting.

I personally believe that Joan Wulff is the best flycaster in America. She began casting as a teenager and eventually won numerous casting tournaments, even against men. At 5 feet 5 inches, some might think her small of stature and ability. But quite the contrary, she is one of the most outstanding athletes around. Now in her 70s, she is still the best. What are you waiting for? Pick up a fly rod and begin to enjoy the exciting world of flyfishing.

Flycasting for Seniors

Though there are numerous flyfishers who qualify for the AARP, very few seniors (age 50 and over) take up the sport. And upon injury or disability, many older people quickly give up the fly as a pastime. In both of these instances, flycasting seems to be the greatest difficulty or hindrance. But by learning some casting shortcuts and even changing some techniques, senior flyfishers can either continue to fish or even take up the fly rod as a new outdoor activity.

At age 40, my eyesight waned. So much for the powers of youth. Add to that a knee that could use some reworking and I almost feel like I'm on the downhill slope. As age creeps up on us, a major flycasting issue is that we begin to lose stamina and casting strength. We've all heard people say, "I just don't have the energy anymore." Some of these ills are real, but many should not limit our time on stream. Let me offer some alternatives to the easy chair, Saturday morning fishing shows, and vicarious stimulation from others' stories.

The right equipment

Our flycasting factoid for the day is "flycasting requires very little strength." I recently witnessed a 3-year-old making decent casts with a 9-foot rod. It was an awesome sight, but it reinforced the fact that strength and power are not necessary for a basic cast.

Now, a senior might not cast for an 8-hour stretch, but two or three hours might be very manageable. Casting with old or antiquated equipment can be part of the problem holding one back. Heavier bamboo or fiberglass rods can cause an outfit to weigh twice as much as modern graphite. Also, a graphite outfit that uses a shorter, lighter rod in possibly a 4-weight instead of a 6-weight can save ounces. Proving this is simple — just go to your local fly shop and compare outfits, or even take your current equipment. It may be shocking to some, but it is easy to save a quarter to a half on outfit weight. Don't dismiss this as trivial. Try to perform any work by lifting twice the weight and you'll instantly be aware of the extra effort. One of my favorite rods is a Sage 0-weight, which is featherlight and surprisingly powerful. On its list of conquests is a 5-pound brown trout and a 6-pound pink salmon, so don't dismiss the diminutive rods as wimpy.

Check two other areas with your setup. Make sure that you have a properly sized grip that does not cause you to squeeze too hard. Something as slight as a "death grip" can be tiring. For elbow pain, a quick fix is to reduce outfit weight or at least change reels. Some of the new, large arbor models are extremely light.

To assist your casting, use **Bear's Casting Aid**. This wrist-stiffening device will correct the floppy-wrist syndrome and tighten your loops. An efficient loop will give you more distance with less effort. For seniors this translates into less false casting and fatigue. As I witness people flycasting on stream, a minimum of half the false casting used is a total waste. The key or secret of good senior flycasting is to conserve energy and effort.

Keeping it simple

It seems as people grow older, life becomes simpler. If this is a principle, it can also be applied to the flyfishing world. Maybe you have flyfished for a lifetime, but I recommend keeping it simple. Don't distance cast (unless you have to); don't double haul; don't use unwieldy sinking lines; don't cast your arm off. Avoiding flyfishing heresy is not my goal in keeping people on the water, so I would like to introduce you to some semi-radical ideas.

First, if you are incapable of casting, troll your fly without casting. Using a small boat, float tube or pontoon craft will get you over the fish. By keeping your fly in the water, you are bound to catch something. Get advice from friends for some of the better waters on which to use this timeless technique.

Another very effective method is to leave your (sinking) fly in the water and practice a jigging action. Almost any streamer or nymph works. My favorite fly for this is a micro-jig. It is deadly on almost any freshwater species of fish. Employing a jigging motion longer will mean a lot less casting.

Even light rods can take big fish. This big brown was caught using a Sage 0-weight.

Try to reduce your casts to those that produce the least shock on your arm and require the least effort. My suggestion is to limit yourself to three basic casts; the pick-up and lay-down, the roll cast and the lob cast. Other chapters discuss these casts, but I want to reemphasize their importance. Spending time perfecting these casts should be the goal of any senior.

The pick-up/lay-down and false cast

The pick-up and lay-down cast limits the need for false casting. With a dry fly, this cast lifts the fly at the end of a downstream drift to be placed upstream again. When fishing with shorter lengths of line, this is almost effortless. Take care not to use more than 25-30 feet of line out. Working longer lines adds to the possibility of unwanted slack or having to strip in some line to get the line pick-up on your rod tip and under control. Making this your primary casting method will reduce your false casting by 50-75 percent. Save energy!

The roll cast

Many people learned roll casting during their initial foray into flyfishing. It is quite simple. Slide the line toward you, pause, then make your forward presentation. Remember, this is half of a regular cast and is missing the backcast phase. Are you getting the picture? With half of a cast, you have reduced your efforts. I enjoy fishing a dry fly directly upstream and repositioning the fly by roll casting. Fishing emergers on a quartering downstream cast also

When the stream is flowing from right to left, the correct hand position for the lob cast is this across-the-body, backhand stance.

takes fish. A roll cast is an easy way to keep your fly in the water. Once on the Cowlitz River in Washington, I hooked dozens of cutthroat trout in a matter of hours with this downstream roll cast. At one point I had landed 20 straight.

The lob cast

Only one more cast to learn on our Keep It Simple flycasting program — the lob cast. No one ever said flycasting always had to be pretty and rhythmic, and the lob cast is ugly and practical. Rigging for this fishing method is done with a strike indicator or with a large dry fly as an indicator above a dropper fly. An 85-year-old friend used a woolly bugger below a large nylon indicator to catch two 20-plus-inch rainbows on Wyoming's Green River. He would begin by roll casting his fly in an upstream fashion, and when the line straightened beneath him, he would jiggle the rod tip to bounce or swim the fly erratically. He would leave the fly in this hangdown position as long as a minute or two. With tension on his fly and line, he would lift the line and lob cast it back upstream. This works well because the fly does not get tangled in the indicator as it will in false casting. Take note again — no false casting, more time fishing, less arm strain.

Seniors should never put their rods on display and hang up their waders one last time because casting has become too difficult. Adjust your equipment and make simple, easy casts that increase your enjoyment and keep you on the water. When I can't cast and flyfish any more, it will be time to stop breathing.

Shaping Up

Rarely, if ever, do you read about ideas for getting into physical condition for flyfishing or flycasting. It is assumed that anyone who can pick up a rod should be able to participate in the sport. That is true. Watching a disabled friend boom long casts from his wheelchair reinforced with me that I could continue flyfishing even with severe limitations. But like almost any other sport, you can be a better flycaster if you work on conditioning.

While the mechanics of casting are not based on power, strength and coordination are extremely helpful. Proper exercising assists in recovering from injury, avoiding injury and building strength and stamina. Have you ever heard of anyone getting hurt from flyfishing? Not often. Fortunately, the work of casting is to swing and propel a 1-pound weight (rod, reel and line) into motion, which is a lot easier and more fun than chopping wood. But tendonitis, arthritis and loss of motor movement can make casting a real pain. Medical attention and miracle drugs can relieve a majority of suffering, but physical therapy and enhancement can remove the impediment.

Exercises

Walking with miniature hand weights produces excellent results for adults. Around age 40, most adults begin to lose muscle mass/weight and replace it with body fat in the wrong places. A walking regimen combined with the slightly taxing effort of hand weights provides an almost total body workout. This general overall body toning facilitates a day's good hiking, wading and casting.

Serious training means a gym workout of stair climbers, stationary bikes, free weights and resistance machines. Flyfishing is probably the least vain of any sport because these newly generated power abs are hidden by waders, vests and fishing jackets. But getting into the best shape possible and staying in condition makes casting easier and more enjoyable.

To build up hand strength, try squeezing a slightly deflated tennis ball or one of the new hand-strengthening gel balls. This squeezing action is also good for your forearm.

The best exercise aid that I have discovered for flycasting is a product called **the Eggsercizer**. Advertised as the world's smallest exercise machine, this resistive hand exerciser is shaped like an egg and fits perfectly into your hand. People use the device for stress reduction, sports strength training, arthritis and injury recovery. Just by squeezing the resilient polymer, a flycaster strengthens fingers, hand, wrist, forearm and elbow. It comes in three densities from soft to firm for different tensioning.

I use the egg to strengthen my casting hand and fingers. With a thumb-on-top grip, you push forward in the cast with your thumb and pull back to the rear with your index finger (for more on this grip, see the section on proper grip in Part 2). You do the same thing by holding the exerciser in your palm with the narrow end pointed up toward the thumb. While squeezing with your last three fingers, push the tip of the egg with your thumb. Remove your index finger from the egg entirely. As you pull back, again squeeze the bottom three fingers, pull hard with your trigger finger, and remove your thumb from the egg. This movement builds powerful hands, fingers and wrists for strong casting. It is a tremendous exercise for conditioning to use 8-weight rods and above in saltwater, salmon and steelhead situations.

A woman holds the Eggsercizer in the starting position for practicing pushing forward in a thumb-on-top grip.

Pantomiming with the egg

One additional practice with the Eggsercizer is to use it with pantomime casting. It fits in your hand like a fat little rod grip. As with basic pantomime casting exercises (for more, see the sections on proper grip and floppy wrists in Part 2), imitate the length and timing of short, medium and long casting strokes. Speed up your tempo. Shoot some casts and do the double haul. I'm driving people crazy at the office. Who says you can't practice flyfishing on the job while reducing stress?

This great little invention can also be chilled in a freezer or heated in hot water and then applied to a stressed or injured area for hot/cold therapy. It is a definite addition to the packing list, although I have refrained from making vest space for it.

30 Days to Better Flycasting is intended to stimulate your thinking and encourage you to "step up" your flyfishing game. By investing part of 30 days in quality exercise and conditioning, your casting will be more enjoyable and comfortable.

Part Two: Beginner

We all have beginning points in any sport. I began flyfishing at age 13. Though a youngster, I had mastered spin fishing and was looking for a new challenge. Watching *The American Sportsman* proclaim the challenge of flyfishing and reading about flies and big fish in *Sports Afield* captured my imagination. It took several month's savings, but I spent $20 at Montgomery Ward for a complete outfit including flies. This was the mid-'60s, and my hard-earned construction money produced a fiberglass rod, heavy automatic reel and a level line. There was no backing. Somehow I knotted the line to the spool and began fishing. Forget casting practice! I went straight to Clear Creek, Arkansas, to tease bass and perch with popping bugs. It was easy, and I caught fish after fish. I know that I never had to cast more than 20 feet and recall that I never let my three brothers go with me for fear of their laughter.

Birth of a passion

On one of those early outings, I fished til dusk. My dad was going to meet me at the main road about a half-mile away at dark. With a few casts left, I placed the bug across stream by an old tree stump. There was a small swirl from my umpteenth perch, but a larger bulge followed and disappeared. I knew a big bass was eager for the bug. Same cast, and boom — an explosion of water and a 2-pound piece of smallmouth dynamite on the other end. It was an epic battle with leaps, jumps and runs. A tired fish came to hand and a flyfisher was born. I have no idea why, but I even released that fish. I guess putting him on the dinner table or waving him under my brothers' noses would have been anti-climactic.

After a hiatus for college and seminary, I resumed flyfishing again. I had long since lost my fly outfit to abuse and a garage sale. My second foray into the sport found me as a terminal beginner. I purchased an early graphite rod and could cast 30 feet. As luck would have it, I caught a rainbow on my first cast. The flames were fanned and I've never stopped since.

My sons were more fortunate and grew up with fly rods in hand. As second-generation flyfishers with a serious flyfishing father, they were fishing at age 5 and entering casting tournaments at 7.

I share these family roots to encourage you in beginning the sport. No matter your age, enjoy your flyfishing and seek to get better. Never be satisfied with average fishing or casting. Master the essentials of casting and enjoy a lifetime of flyfishing experiences.

The Proper Grip

One of the very basic aspects of good casting is keeping your body in the proper position and holding your rod correctly. As I teach clinics around the country and evaluate casting-instructor candidates, I find that a majority of people hold or grip the rod with an inefficient, if not erroneous, style. This may not be a critical error if you are pitching a nymph 20 feet on some small stream, but if you need to beat the wind on Montana's Yellowstone River or make a distance cast on Utah's Green, a proper grip is imperative.

Grip styles

The one grip that causes the most problems is called a **"V" grip**. A neophyte flyfisher will pick up a fly rod much like a golf club or a baseball bat by completely wrapping all his fingers around the rod. This forms a "V" on the top of the rod. Particularly on the backcast, the rod will fall through this space in the "V" and allow the rod to drop too low to the rear. When this happens, a large, weak loop is formed and, most typically, your line piles up 15 to 20 feet in front of you.

Changing from this free-wrist "V" grip to another style usually is a step toward resolving this casting ill. Another grip places the index finger (forefinger) on top of the rod and, logically, is called the **index** or **forefinger grip**. This grip is helpful because it allows you to point your finger toward the casting target. Using an index grip with a 3- or 4-weight rod for creek fishing works fine for accurate, short-range casts. You will find, however, that this grip does not give you much hand or index-finger strength and is almost useless on rods heavier than a 6-weight. On heavier rods an index grip will lead to a tired hand and sloppy casting.

The primary grip used by most experienced flycasters is the **thumb** or **thumb-on-top grip**. To perform this grip, grasp the rod with your thumb centered on top of the handle while spreading your remaining fingers underneath.

But even the best of casters lose efficiency by not cocking the thumb on the grip and/or not placing the index finger directly opposite the thumb on the underside.

Here is a free casting clinic tip: Take your thumb and lay it flat across your opposite wrist. Press your thumb down firmly in this flattened position. Next, cock or flex your thumb up so that you can see a space under the middle of the thumb and the pad of the thumb presses directly into your wrist. Apply the same pressure. You have about three or four times the strength! That strength is translated into extra power for driving the rod forward in forceful casting situations.

Soggy practice for a firm grip

Now that you have tested your strength with this thumb grip, let's use it in a pantomime session. Joan Salvato Wulff, one of America's great casting instructors, teaches students to squeeze a sponge and imitate this grip during casting. So go get a larger sponge out of the kitchen and wet it. Using the proper grip with the cocked/flexed thumb on top and index finger opposite, you are going to imitate your casting stroke. Push your hand in a straight line to the front. You should gently squeeze until the stop at the end of your stroke. At the stop, you should make a tighter squeeze as your thumb presses forward to add speed. At this point, your index finger acts as a stop or point of resistance. On the backcast, do just the opposite. The index finger supplies the force and the thumb serves as the stop. As you practice, you should be wringing water from the sponge at the end of each stroke. Also, notice that you are not holding the sponge in a death grip and squeezing water throughout. This is the same as real casting. Your hand should be slightly relaxed during the middle of your stroke. If your spouse thinks you are crazy doing this, make up some excuse about cleaning the floor.

One last grip to learn — my favorite — is called the **thumb and forefinger grip** or the **combination grip**. People who use this grip stumble onto it by accident and think that they invented it. Gary Borger uses it and fell upon it from routine casting. The reason that it is such a good grip is that it places your hand, wrist

30 *Days to Better Flycasting* BEGINNER | 49

Bear demonstrates holding the rod in a solid, thumb-on-top grip.

and forearm in their most natural position during casting with the least amount of twisting or strain. From the center of the rod, your thumb is held slightly off center and slightly flexed, along with your forefinger (index) held on the upper outside of the rod (almost on top) and barely flexed. Your other three fingers are used to hold underneath the rod. Lower your arm and raise it naturally from your side to waist high. Look at your hand. It is formed into a natural gripping position. I can use this grip for everything but the heaviest of rods, when I switch to thumb on top.

Final points on grip

A few final points before I turn you loose for practice. You must grip the rod as far to the rear of the handle as is comfortable or possible. This is a trick for distance casters that is based on good physics. Everyone has heard about buying a balanced fly outfit, but you must balance this rod/lever in your hand. Your reel with line spooled on weighs twice as much as your rod. By placing your hand near the reel, you offset the weight and allow the rod to bend more deeply. I have seen some people hold their rod at the top of the grip and even grasp the graphite. This is OK for your 15- to 20-foot cast; after that, it is a waste of good rod energy.

Not only is rod grip important, but make sure the grip shape and size work for you. This is a critical point for youth and women. Before you select your rod of a lifetime, test the grip size and comfort.

If you want to reach the top of your game, exercise your hand strength (see the section in Part One called "Shaping Up").

I know many of you were laughing at me when I talked about the importance of your rod grip style. But a proper grip can add five feet of distance for most casters. When flyfishing is sometimes said to be a game of inches, I am happy to have some extra feet available.

Poetry in Motion:
Using the Correct Body Position

Have you heard of "excess body?" No, I am not referring to being an overweight flyfisher, but rather to too much body movement, which can be a detriment to good flycasting. Also, putting your body and arms in the wrong positions can strangle any hope of ever becoming a solid caster. Body control is foundational for building the proper basic approach to any and all good casting.

In my years on the casting circuit, I have watched the top 1 percent of American gurus ply their trade before enraptured audiences. With gaping mouths, we have all been amazed at the fluidity and poetry of Joan Wulff, Mel Krieger, Lefty Kreh, Gary Borger and others as they worked their magic wands. If you deconstruct any single cast they make, you will find that it is made with maximum efficiency and the least wasted motion and energy. Their basis for "looking good," which we also need to master, comes as we set for ourselves the personal goal of turning our casting into poetry in motion.

Commit to reaching your peak

Every day we watch sporting events and view some truly amazing feats. We are awestruck to see Karl Malone gyrate with a basketball. Tiger Woods leaves us shaking our heads and thinking, "How did he do that?" Like our other professional athletes, professional flyfishers have worked for years to perfect their game. Dedicating ourselves to the proposition that we are going to become better or even excellent flycasters is the starting point. Then, all you have to say is that you are going to take the rest of your life to achieve that goal.

Flyfishers and casters come in all shapes and sizes, male and female, young and old. We are all blessed or cursed with some measure of coordination and athletic ability. Since most of us are in the average category, it is nice to know that being middle-of-the-road is all it takes. However (this is a definite qualification), flycasting does require that we use the best of our physical ability and mental concentration to achieve our peak level.

A beginning

Let's get started. Before you begin casting, make sure your casting arm is loose and relaxed. Regular exercises and stretching will keep your shoulder, elbow, wrist and hand in top shape. Work on strengthening your grip. Just squeezing a tennis ball is all it takes. As much as 20 percent of your casting power and quickness is transmitted through your hand. Arm strength is a help, but not critical. I have never seen a master caster who was pumped up like a weightlifter.

And of course, one of the very best methods for getting in condition for flycasting is to cast a great deal! In the West, we get in shape for skiing by skiing. A mistake many people make is that they do not prepare for the physical aspect of the game. I am not requiring that you hone yourself to the razor's edge, but you have to be physically ready and overcome any weaknesses.

Many people start off on the wrong foot because of poor equipment or an unbalanced outfit. Some examples are women or children using a rod that is too heavy or that has too large a grip. Other people use rods that do not fit their casting style and cause problems. I have seen people try to fish on windy Yellowstone Lake with a 5-weight rod, a feat that is almost impossible. Knowledgeable friends and fly shop pros will generally steer you straight on equipment.

Let's try to take a snapshot of a person who has difficulty keeping their correct basic body positioning. For most fishing and casting situations, begin with your feet aimed square to your target (the place where you want your fly to land). If you are not square to the target, you must twist your upper body to bring the target back in line. Although I will wade and cast at the same time, for the most part you want to keep your feet still. It is common for people to have their feet spread widely and with one or the other to the rear. This is not good for balance and leads to a rocking body motion. A good athletic stance, with feet squared and shoulder-width apart, works for casting. Try to imitate a blue heron that is very still and deliberate in its motion.

Your torso does not figure into casting that much. Like your feet, keep your lower and upper body oriented toward the target.

Practicing to start a basic cast: Wrist locked, shoulders square to target, and elbow lowered and slightly away from the body.

Throwing your body back and forth to assist the back and fore stroke in your cast only wastes energy. An awkward rocking motion can be caused by improper pulling of the line with the line hand. Keep the body under control and steady.

Positioning the arm and elbow

Our primary problem area is where to position our arm during casting. I cringe when I see a flycaster lift his elbow high with his casting hand far above the head. Do this for me. Reach overhead with an invisible rod in hand and make 10 false casts. Ouch! The pain goes right to your shoulder. When you do that for a half-day, you are almost ready for the hospital. It is extremely difficult to control and time your cast with the rod held high. With this position, it is also very hard to power your rod with a good speed up and stop.

Most good casting places your elbow slightly removed from your side. This allows for freedom of movement since the elbow moves to the front and rear during casting. How far? The elbow moves a small distance for a short stroke and a longer path for a long stroke or distance cast. If your cast is made on a tilted plane, either aiming low or high in front, the elbow must move on this angled path to achieve the correct cast. As an example, to make a parachute cast that ends with your line high to the front, you must angle your rod low to the rear and finish high in the front. This means that your elbow tracks from low in the rear to high in the front as well.

Americans adopted flyfishing from their English brethren. On southern England chalk streams, where fishers only cast to rising trout, the elbow is locked to the side of the body to provide for a highly accurate upstream cast. The casts are short and pinpoint. Rarely do colonists have the luxury of staying short. With changing direction, mending and seeking distance, an elbow-out position is more versatile.

Another mistake is made in the movement of the shoulder during casting. A correct motion follows a straight line or 180-degree path. This tracking also keeps your fly line moving in the same plane. The problem stems from rolling your shoulder in a 270-degree path to the outside. This happens when some casters have an uncontrolled sidearm cast. Your rod and line follow this shoulder movement and the line ends up behind and past your opposite shoulder. By taking your cast out of plane, the result is an underpowered cast with a curve at the front upon delivery. Stop! I know people who have cast this way all their lives. In their effort to keep the flies away from themselves with this sideward rotation, these fishers have cut their casting range and ability effectively in half.

Using the video age

How can we work on fluidity of movement in casting? Today, most people have access to a video camera. Film yourself doing a variety of casting: short casts, long, hauling and presentation casts. Most of the full service fly shops have video/TV units and can give you an on-the-spot evaluation. You can also take casting lessons. It is just like a tune-up for the car or going to the dentist — lessons are needed to get things in good shape and iron out problems. With time and effort, your casting will transform into poetry in motion.

Casting's No. 1 Problem: The Floppy Wrist

It was another great day to be on the middle section of the Provo River. The guys at Trout Bum 2 were all singing praise about the golden stones and green drakes, which were providing a "full meal deal" hatch. A group of us tested the fishing and found it challenging. High water and a pretty stiff breeze required us to use our best casting skills. Some fish were caught on a short line, but others demanded a 40-foot cast. As I switched positions, I watched other fishers work their lies (the place where fish hold, not the size of the fish they would report later). I noticed that many flies never reached target because of a common casting error: the floppy wrist. These "wrist casters" were not only having to work hard at their casting, but were hardly catching anything. With a greedy thought, I figured "more fish for me."

Advancing in flycasting skills is not always easy, and a huge roadblock is casting with a loose or floppy wrist. People cannot advance beyond a basic intermediate level unless they cure the dreaded ill of a hinging/flexing wrist. This problem will give you more frustration than any other mistake in casting.

Pinpointing the wrist

Just what is this floppy (bending) wrist? If I were to highlight the wrist during the casting motion, you would see it fall over to the back and front as if the fisher is hitchhiking. When the butt end of the rod moves more than 45 degrees away from your wrist, you have bent the wrist too much.

On the forward and backward casting stroke, the hand, wrist and forearm propel the rod into an arc, which in turn directs the fly line and fly toward a target. Correct casting demands that the rod itself do most of the work. A loose wrist directs the rod tip over a large curved path that produces low line energy and a weak cast. The rod tip dips too low to the back and front, resulting in a large, open loop or even worse, a non-loop. Casting a large loop causes the line energy to be directed outward and downward, and the final delivery cast piles up in front of the caster and will not straighten. The weak, floppy wrist cast shows itself in the line piling up in front of you like this or in never being able to cast much more than 30 feet.

If the wrist is not flexed (or if flexing is held to a minimum), you will get a smaller loop that pushes most of the line energy to the rear and front. This makes an efficient, effective cast. Upon presentation, the line will straighten neatly to the front and tug at your line hand, showing that the line has extra power to release and shoot. A stiffened/locked wrist allows the forearm to become an extension of the rod and do more of the work.

Practice methods

I was stuck with this wrist problem for years. In the past, slow, flexible parabolic action rods contributed to the floppy wrist. But current graphite rods allow you to overcome the problem more easily. And to become a truly good caster, you must stop bending your wrist.

Jokingly, but truthfully, I'll tell you that I learned to flycast in a car. One of the best ways to learn casting is to pantomime. By holding your index finger upward like a miniature rod, you can push your hand to the front and rear imitating a casting stroke. With a short stroke comes a short cast; a longer push results in a distance cast. Try to time your movements to an actual casting rhythm. Make sure that you keep a stiff wrist. It should not bend. Proof of a good stroke is that your finger will track in a straight line without tipping to the front or back. When you stop at a light in the car, try getting in a dozen casts. You may look strange, but you'll notice results immediately.

Another method for preventing the dreaded flexing wrist is to do some casting practice with Bear's Casting Aid. Attached to the butt end of your rod, it will stiffen your wrist and keep the rod from pivoting more than 45 degrees. You can also fish with the Aid to keep tighter loops.

For practice, put on your Casting Aid and position your hand on the rod grip right above your reel. Trap the line under the fingers of your rod hand. This is going to feel very awkward during your initial practice strokes. However, as you false cast, this tight feel is very close to a correct position, which you will achieve later without the Aid. If you look up at your rod tip during this exercise, it will be moving in a straight line, which means your casting energy is being driven properly to the front and rear.

Practice makes perfect

Thousands of flyfishers suffer from floppy wrist syndrome. Pills won't help and neither can a psychiatrist. You must get out on the lawn and do these practice exercises to groove the correct cast. Flycasting is the name of the game. The better you get means the better your fishy results.

As I mentioned earlier, a tight, locked wrist helps produce tight casting loops. We needed these tight loops to cast into the sea breezes at Christmas Island in the Pacific. Unless you locked your wrist and drove your cast into the wind, you practically had to give up fishing or fish at your feet. I just bet that 5-pound bonefish wished that I hadn't practiced casting in the Jeep!

Floppy wrist syndrome is caused by rotating the rod butt more than 45 degrees away from the wrist, like this.

Getting the Slack Out

It was a hot, humid, sweaty day in Virginia and I was tired. A steady stream of flycasters, young and old, male and female, had made it over to the casting lawn, and lessons had been going nonstop. As it turned out, over 600 people received free casting lessons from Team Sage at Camp Jeep, the national family outdoors retreat sponsored by Jeep Corporation every August. Most people were beginning casters and had trouble forming good casting loops and keeping their wrists from bending. Another casting mistake was that everyone (yes, 600 out of 600) was allowing slack to creep into their casts. I'm afraid most of us aren't much different from the Camp Jeepers, so let's give some attention to this casting problem.

Slack is a sag, bend or curve in the fly line before and during casting. You cannot make a correct cast without a loaded (properly bent) rod tip. This loading move allows the rod to bend more fully during the power stroke portion of the cast. Slack attacks during loading and powering.

Basic training

Have any of you attended a flycasting clinic? Quite often the casting instructor will bark instructions at you like a drill sergeant. Two important commands that I issue are "line straight" and "rod tip low — six inches!" Getting the basics straight helps in getting the slack out. An additional directive that I give intermediate casters is "get your hands together."

Beginning casters are particularly frustrated when their line piles up at the completion of a forecast. If you try to make another cast with all of that curvy line to the front, you will blow the next cast as well. What is happening is that the rod will not load until the line comes straight and the rod tip bends. To correct this first slack mistake, strip in line until it is straight in front of you, then begin your cast. As you lift the rod, notice that the rod begins to load immediately. You are now in position to make a good cast.

Here, a short amount of line is held securely in the line hand, which rests at about the maximum distance you want it from the rod hand.

A second slack error can creep into your cast and is almost unnoticeable. It comes from starting the cast with your rod held too high. Holding the rod tip high is a carryover from spin fishing for most anglers. Certainly, if you are holding the rod with the tip at waist level or above, you have added slack. Arguing will do you little good because proof is in the casting. Even minor amounts of slack can ruin a cast. Lower the rod tip to six inches off the ground or water. With a low rod tip, your rod is bending and loading below waist level. It is easy then to power the rod normally.

Improper use of the line hand and where it is held contributes to a final slack mistake. I was made aware of this several years ago as I began casting for Sage Rod Company. Geoff was 13 at the time and made a snide comment during a TV fishing show. Sure enough, the governor of Idaho was throwing all kinds of slack with his hands held widely apart. When I see the line hand held much more than six inches from the rod hand, problems are sure to happen. Even intermediate flycasters have difficulty getting this right. Slack, in this case, is the amount of loose line from the line hand to the stripping guide (the first one) on the rod. Sometimes three or even four feet of line is being scissored during false casting. Even six inches to a foot of uncontrolled slack injected into a false cast can mess up the whole enchilada.

Once you are aware of the slack problem associated with widely separated hands, you will spot it in a minute in other flycasters. Watch your friends cast. It may look like traditional casting to keep your hands apart, but it is not functional. Spend some time thumbing through your favorite flyfishing magazines. Try to spot those hands-apart casters who are letting slack sneak into the cast.

Applying the lesson

How about a quick casting clinic: Get out in the yard and start with your first two slack reducers, line straight and rod tip low. Next, begin false casting with about 30 feet of line out. To keep your hands from separating, bring your line hand up against your rod hand. Pretend that your two hands are welded together. This feels awkward but provides the correct movement for the line hand. Again, as you false cast, both hands should be moving in tandem. For the actual casting motion, separate your hands to no more than six to 12 inches apart and continue with a good false-casting sequence. The slack is gone.

I frequently talk about adding distance to your cast. Getting the slack out is one of the best techniques for maintaining a powerful stroke to provide distance or to overcome windy conditions. Once you control the slack problem, you are well on your way to mastering the basic fundamentals of good casting.

Part Three: Intermediate

There is no magic hurdle that you must cross to reach an intermediate standard, and you don't wake up some morning to the realization that you are a full-fledged, better than the average flyflinger. For me, the line stopped piling up in the front, and I could release line on my presentation cast and it would shoot to the target. I even found my equipment did not fit anymore, so I saved every penny to purchase a top-of-the-line rod blank, which transformed into a handsome wand. As fortune and Uncle Sam would have it, I was promptly transferred to Germany for a five-year tour.

In an effort to learn to speak German, I began studying their flyfishing magazines and attended a flycasting course. Through stumbling German and broken English, the instruction proved to be an immense help. My money spent on casting lessons was as valuable as my expenditure on gear. For the next half-decade, I was able to enjoy casting and fishing on Europe's best waters. It was tough duty, but somebody had to do it. Ha!

Breaking free from the sometimes terminal grip of beginnerdom isn't always easy. I know casters in their 50s, 60s and 70s who are still flailing and flopping away. My best advice is to get help. Ask for lessons for Christmas. Many fly shops offer free seminars. Once you progress up the skills ladder, your far-away fishing adventures will be a lot more meaningful.

Roll Casting for Results

One of the very best casts for both youth and adults is the roll cast. At ages 9 and 5, my sons, Geoff and Ty, fished with me on a private stream in Germany. They were nailing grayling on about every cast with Griffith's gnats, and our German friends were awed by their roll-casting abilities and fish-catching results.

A roll cast is used whenever there is an obstruction behind you that will not allow a full backcast. If you are flyfishing in a drift boat, the bow caster must roll cast to reposition the fly. Without a roll, everyone else in the boat had better keep low! A roll cast is also good for lengthening line before regular casting.

While wading the Deschutes, a roll cast is imperative to overcome the willows and cottonwoods that eat a backcast. If you wade upstream on your favorite river and punch out 25-foot roll casts, you can cover almost every holding and feeding lie. Think of all of the mountain streams in Pennsylvania that are choked with streamside bushes and trees. Sometimes a roll cast is the only possible method of reaching fish.

The stop/pause position in a roll cast: With the line anchored in the water, the caster is ready to make the forward power stroke.

It is amazing that many people never learn to roll cast properly. Sometimes you just can't get any distance, or the line piles up in front, or the line slaps the water so hard that fish scatter. The corrections for roll-casting mistakes are very simple and exact. Anyone can become an expert roll caster.

Breaking down the cast

Let's analyze a cast and get everything in order. It is best to practice roll casting on water because it is water tension gripping the fly line that loads the rod. Try to find a pond, swimming pool or slow-moving stream as a practice site. Now, get your body position correct. Typically, you stand square to the target; in roll casting you drop the foot matching your casting hand to the rear to form an open stance. That means a right-handed caster will step a foot length or two to the rear with the right foot. This opens the shoulder for better movement and distance as the rod is pulled to the rear and the forecast is made. The starting position is like a normal cast — line straight and rod tip low. After drawing or pulling the line toward you, the cast is powered to the front like any normal cast. A little extra power is needed to break the line free from the water. The loop that forms is elliptical in shape and resembles a flattened circle. This differs from the "U" or "V" shape of a regular casting loop.

There are some critical points in roll casting that must be mastered. Not stopping the rod and anchoring the line is the most typical mistake with this cast. As you draw the line toward you by lifting your casting hand, you must stop the rod and pause when the rod comes to a nearly vertical position overhead. The rod position is cocked slightly to the rear, allowing the line to fall a little behind your shoulder. In casting clinics, I wait for as long as 30 seconds to prove that this stop is necessary and effective. Again, this pause allows the water to grip the line, which bends the rod on the forecast.

Check the location of your hand as the cast is made. The rod can be driven to the front more easily when the rod hand is lifted face or head high. In roll casting, casters have the tendency to leave their casting hands low. A way to check your hand position is to look to the side when you stop the rod on the drawback movement. If you have it right, you will be looking directly at your reel.

Sometimes your line will either slap into the rod or crash into itself on the forward cast. To avoid this mistake, you must tilt or angle the rod tip away from you as it comes to vertical. The rod tilts slightly to the rear and to the outside. At this point, the line will drop off the rod tip and loop down from slightly behind you into the water. Take care that the line doesn't catch itself on the tip as you come to this position. When you cast to the front, aim to the left or inside of the line which is still lying on the water to the front. Your final aim should also be on the intended target. The direction in which we speed up and stop the rod is the direction the line will take.

This good roll cast features the right foot spaced to the rear; a good, high rod hand position and a close line hand; and a tilted rod with the line looping to the rear.

Two more final mistakes can still ruin our cast. Don't hinge your wrist as you come forward. Keep the wrist locked and drive the rod tip forward in a straight line. If you hinge the wrist, you'll lose power and your loop will look more like a circle. Practice with your Casting Aid to avoid this. Also, do not lower the rod toward the water as you power it to the front. This causes both line pileup and a big splash. Your prize fish will be headed to the bottom when that happens.

Tips on practicing

As I have mentioned before, any cast that can be made with a rod can be made in pantomime. Pretend you have your invisible rod in your hand. I like to do this in my office chair at work as a form of stress relief. Be sure to warn your co-workers or they'll think

This roll cast has two problems: The hand is poorly positioned in front of the body, and the line does not loop to the rear behind the rod.

you've lost it. First, go through the roll casting sequence slowly to make sure you have everything in the proper place. As you master it, begin making regular casts. Also, go practice on your local pond. Finally, try to teach one other person this cast. You'll be

30 Days to Better Flycasting

INTERMEDIATE | 67

amazed how you improve when you teach others. This is the easiest cast to teach, learn and master for all ages, male or female.

A couple of pointers for advanced casters. You can make a longer roll cast by making a single haul as you come to the front. Also, by reaching farther to the rear with your casting hand, you can lengthen your stroke for more distance. Another tip is that a roll cast can be made to your backhand or offhand. The secret is to tilt your head and position your casting hand above your head. Do not try to backhand roll cast by positioning your casting arm or hand underneath your chin. Your cast ends up very restricted.

An underpowered roll cast or one delivered with a loose wrist flops weakly to the front like this.

If you perfect the roll cast, you can become a very good flycaster. You will find that it is one of your favorite casts and that you will use it on almost every fishing adventure.

Troubled Loops

Crack! The loud noise sounded like a gunshot and turned me from my fishing focus at Wyoming's Monster Lake. What had happened? One of our fishing friends began to wade to shore with a hand covering his face. He had just launched a lead-eyed Clouser minnow into his glasses at about 55 MPH. Needless to say, the glasses didn't exist anymore. The friend was only a bit shaken and was able to resume fishing later, but it was almost a serious casting accident. He later pulled aside Geoff, my 18-year-old son and a certified casting instructor, to ask for casting lessons. I overheard our friend ask, "How can you control your fly line in all of this wind?"

An excellent question! The reason that most casters have problems with accuracy and distance is that they cannot control their casting loops. Thus, they suffer from troubled loops.

The **casting loop** is the shape that the line takes as it comes off your rod tip on your fore (front) and back (backwards/behind) casts. It looks like a "U" or at the end of a cast a "J" on its side. A big or large loop is called an **open loop**. In contrast, a small or narrow loop is called a **tight loop**. If you underpower the fly rod while casting and flop the line to the back and front in powerless fashion without letting the line unfurl, you can even get a **nonloop**. A final loop — one of casting's worst mistakes — is the **tailing loop**. This erroneous loop usually results in a tangled cast because the top leg of the casting loop dips below the bottom, sometimes snagging itself or tying itself into a wind knot.

So what's the big deal about troubled loops? Unless we learn to control and adjust our casting loops, we will have trouble casting weighted flies and casting in a wind, and we will never reach our maximum distance.

Practicing varying loops

Let's begin with an open loop. To make this wide loop, the rod is allowed to follow a larger arc and to drop slightly to the front and rear. Do not abruptly stop the rod. This open loop

INTERMEDIATE | 69

allows you to cast heavy or weighted flies and keep them away from you and your rod. Fly rods are very durable, but hit one with a weighted fly or a sharp hook point and you will test your warranty.

It's time for casting practice. You should be able to vary the size of your casting loop. Start by dropping your rod far to the rear and then to the front while false casting. You'll have a very large loop. Tighten it up a bit by lowering the rod from its vertical position by only 45 degrees each direction. Your wide loop will have decreased in size. Try one more time and rotate the rod downward by another 20 or 30 degrees. Again, your loop is more normal looking. For casting graduate students, go through this same exercise, but do it to your backhand.

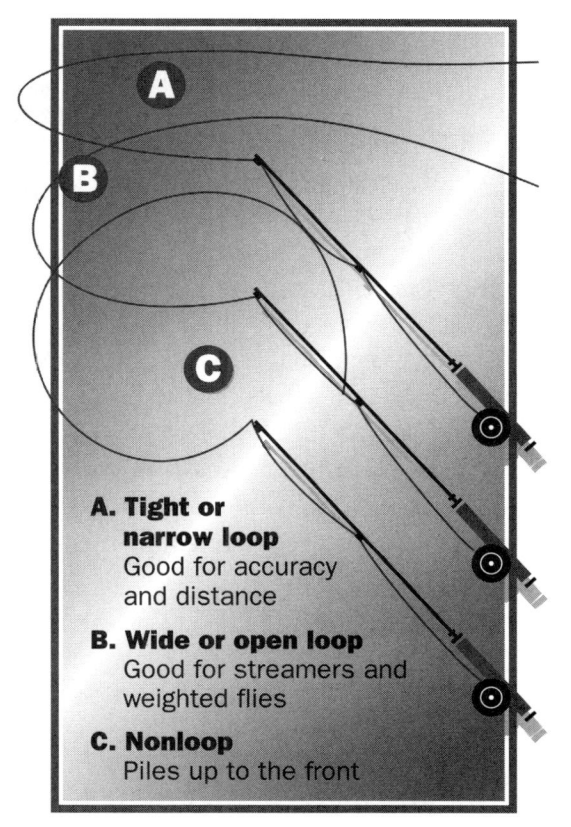

Some people have a horrible time trying to cast a narrow loop. If you have ever tried fishing for bass and bluegill, you will understand the importance of a tight loop. Because the fish lie on the edge of the weeds, you must accurately place your fly on their food table. I watched Randi Swisher of Sage Rods win the International Sportsman's Exhibition Casting Accuracy Contest, beating out 600 other contestants, by forming a very tight casting loop and hovering his yarn over the target. He registered the only perfect score.

A. Tight or narrow loop
Good for accuracy and distance

B. Wide or open loop
Good for streamers and weighted flies

C. Nonloop
Piles up to the front

Mastering the tight loop

How do you produce a tight loop? The faster you speed up and then stop the rod during the power phase of your casting stroke, the narrower loop you will form. This short acceleration to a stop causes the rod tip to arc slightly to form a tight loop. This calls for powering your rod in a straight-line path and not having a floppy wrist. I have never seen anyone make narrow casting loops without practicing and, in some cases, taking lessons.

Getting the proper feel is critical for learning. Pretend that you are going to hammer a nail that is at eye level to your front and another to your back. Drive your invisible hammer forward and stop suddenly at the head of the nail. You just made a casting stroke with a speed up and stop. Now start with your hammer at the front and drive backward to hit another nail. Put the two together and you are now forming a tight loop. Another practice exercise is to take an apple or orange and plunge it onto the top of a paint stirring stick (or you can use the bottom half of your $400 graphite fly rod — just kidding). Go out to the yard and fling the fruit off. Try to get some distance. It works best when you speed up and stop the stick. Just like casting!

One of the difficulties in getting the right feel for casting is that there are very few other instances where we power our hand to the rear as we do in a backcast. But it is close to the snap throw made by a catcher in baseball.

Gaining more control

OK, some of you are now casting nice, pretty, narrow loops. If you want to gain more loop control in your casting, try this. This is called "Doing the 180." The object is to control your casting loop by doing your false casting within a 180-degree arc from sidearm front to sidearm back. Start by casting directly sidearm to your strong side. Make two false casts with a narrow loop. Without stopping, move the arc upward about 30 degrees and make two more. Again, controlling your loops, move to a 3/4 position or higher. Continue making two casts and move to a forehand vertical (straight overhead or overhand). Move to backhand vertical, backhand 3/4, backhand 30, and backhand

Bear casts while sitting in a park. Practicing while sitting forces you to tighten your loops and simulates float tube fishing.

sidearm. If you are at a master level of casting, continue Doing the 180 until you blow the cast.

An exercise for float tubers or pontoon craft fishing is to Do the 180 while sitting down. This is much like the low position in the water. If you make big, open loops, the line will touch the ground behind you. In real fishing, this is the ripping sound of the fly landing and being extracted from the backcast. Doing the 180 makes you focus on the tightest loop possible.

I hope you are getting some helpful ideas from these casting exercises. Keep at it. Make your mantra, "More tight loops. More tight loops." With practice, you will improve.

The Infamous Tailing Loop

It was a sad and tragic sight. Broken, shattered, crushed... the rod reflected the man. His downcast look was one of someone who had just lost his best friend. He kept muttering, "I didn't mean to. I didn't mean to." I'm afraid to say that this terminal accident happens more frequently than anyone would want: Our flyfishing friend had slammed a weighted streamer into his upper rod and demolished it. By trying to get maximum distance on his cast, he had been tailing his casting loop, which dropped the fly into his rod. I couldn't help but identify with his loss, though I knew it was doubly painful for him because I continued to catch Alaskan sockeye left and right.

I guess that one good reason to change our behavior and actions is avoidance of pain. I know this is true in marriage counseling. In flyfishing, whether it is a broken rod or knotted leaders resulting in lost fish, correcting our tailing loops should be high on our list. My worst incident was fishing an evening bite on a Montana lake. The fish were crazy, with a strike on every cast. Light was fading when I put my line all over my rod in a tangled mess. Quitting was my only option after such a tailing fiasco. Sure, some flyfishers can advance to an intermediate level with tailing loops, but they'll never progress beyond.

Defining the problem

A **tailing loop** is formed when the top portion of the line in a loop, whether front or rear, falls below the bottom leg of the loop. In fishing, this tailing loop usually includes line, leader and fly, and all are subject to tangles. The tailing loop can tie an overhand knot in the line or leader known as a wind knot. It is not caused by the wind, however, but by bad casting. When a friend lost a good fish on the Green River on one occasion, I noticed that his leader was covered with these tailing loop knots. Weakening the leader and tippet could mean losing the fish of a lifetime.

Just what causes a tailing loop? The primary reason for tailing loops is the wrong application of power during the casting

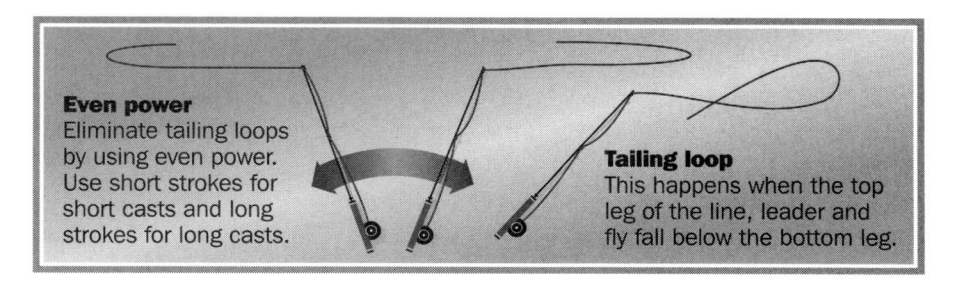

Even power
Eliminate tailing loops by using even power. Use short strokes for short casts and long strokes for long casts.

Tailing loop
This happens when the top leg of the line, leader and fly fall below the bottom leg.

sequence. An early or premature powering of the rod during the loading phase will cause the rod to bend then relax, tracking the rod in a dipping or concave arc. Remember that fly line always follows the direction of the rod tip, so a concave movement pulls the upper leg of your loop downward into a tailing loop. This concave movement can also be caused by lowering your hand as you begin your cast then lifting during your power stroke.

A friend of mine throws beautiful tailing loops. He uses a short stroke and applies power with a strong wrist snap. As he approaches longer casting lengths with over 40 feet of line, this short, rapid application of power does not allow the line to travel smoothly to the front or rear. The cause of this tailing loop is that too short of a casting stroke is being made to cast a long line.

Beginners have a particular problem with unequal power. They will lift the rod weakly in an underpowered backcast, then hammer or overpower the fly rod to the front to try to lay out line. The top leg of the loop drops to hook over the bottom almost every time.

Lefty Kreh has another explanation for tailing loops made by advanced casters. Casting tight loops by driving your rod in a straight-line path can also cause your trailing line to crash into the forward part of your loop. This happens with an extremely stiff wrist that locks the rod on one track.

Addressing the situation

Let's fix or at least improve on our tailing loop dilemma. Practice a smooth application of the power stroke at all casting distances from short to long. Avoid any abrupt powering and stopping. It is also a big help to apply equal power to the front and rear. I call this flyfishing math. One plus one equals one. A good backcast with the proper application of power along with equal power on the forecast produces a good overall presentation sans tailing loop. Also, adjust your casting stroke length to the length or distance that you cast. Short cast, short stroke; long cast, long stroke.

Lefty's tailing issue is corrected by very slightly pushing and pulling down the rod tip to front and back. When you move the tip this distance of "a frog's whisker," your loop is pulled open a fraction and causes the top leg to pass over the bottom.

Check out your equipment as well. Fast-action rods are less susceptible to tailing than soft or moderate rods. The general tendency is to power a soft rod more than the quick tip movement in a faster action or taper.

The best casters have learned to tame the tailing loop. Don't give up on yourself. If you have to, completely relearn your casting. With fewer tangles and wind knots, you'll get to enjoy the big one that didn't get away.

Learning to Shoot

My boys took their required hunter safety class as they were learning to duck hunt. They spent countless hours in shooting practice and in the class itself. With the right instruction and preparation, they were ready for the challenge of the real thing. In flycasting, learning to shoot is almost as critical and integral as in hunting. **Shooting line** is the method of releasing extra loose line with your line hand into your false cast so that you can lengthen your cast for more distance. Unless you want to restrict your fishing to a 25-foot limit, you must learn to shoot line properly. When I watch people flail the air with their flycasting at the outdoors sports shows, I know that their fishing must be suffering as well. Shooting line correctly is just as important as proper breathing in shooting. This lesson will focus on how to practice for good results.

Let me present a dismal picture of Joe and Jane Flycaster, who are beating the air with their fly rods and not getting their cast to do much except land in a messy pile on delivery. Their rod paints a wide arc, with the line passing in big loops, and when they release line from their line hand to make extra distance, they almost rip their shorts with futile effort. The line still doesn't travel much farther on the cast, they are a lot more tired, and often the line itself gets tangled over the butt end of the rod or smashes up against the stripping guide and kills the whole cast. Another thing Joe and Jane try (and they'll do almost anything out of desperation) is to use their line hand to push line up to the guide, almost hoping to thread it through and out the end.

Beginning to fix the picture

Shooting line correctly requires timing, smooth powering of the rod and proper use of the line hand. Intermediate flycasters must learn how to shoot line. Again, by building on the basic foundation of good casting mechanics, shooting line is a natural progression. The critical skills that are needed are a good pick-up of line from the water to begin the cast; good false casting, with the rod properly loaded; and good, tight loops that will propel the forecast and pull extra line through the guides upon delivery.

In your practice session, you can work on a technique that is close to a spinning rod cast. First, begin a series of false casts with 25-30 feet of line extended from the rod tip. Take the loose line below the stripping guide and trap it underneath the index and middle fingers of your rod hand. Pull off five to 10 feet of extra line from your reel and leave it in a pile away from your feet. This is the line that will be used during shooting. Place your line hand in your pants pocket. Do not use it during this exercise! Start your casting sequence and feel the line on the rod. Watch your loops to be sure that they have the best look. To shoot the line, you want to release the trapped line on the forward cast once you have stopped your rod on the forecast and a good loop is beginning to form off the rod tip. This is very similar to a spinning rod cast where you release line from your finger on the forward cast.

It is elementary when you make a good shooting cast because the extra line will be pulled from the ground into the rod guides and exit out the rod tip. Your cast will extend from the 25-30 feet up to 35-40 feet. Keep practicing this until you smooth things out and the line jumps off the rod. There may be some problems with the line hitting the first guide or wrapping around the rod shaft. We can fix those problems with our next practice session. Before you advance, try being more aggressive with your casting stroke. Add some speed. Continue to shoot line and you'll find that the line shoots out more quickly and for longer distance.

Mastering the line hand

Our next activity is used to train your line hand to maximize its function. First, grip the line with your line hand by pinching it between your thumb and first two fingers. Strip off extra line to shoot as before while dropping it at your feet. Positioning your hand during the cast is critical. If your line hand drops under and behind your rod hand during the casting stroke and line release, there is a good chance that the line will cross and tangle over the butt end of the rod. We all make this casting mistake and it is a pain in the —. When you practice this time, keep the line hand within six to 12 inches of the rod hand and stay even or slightly in front of it. Upon release, the line is positioned to the front of the butt end and becomes almost impossible to tangle. Go through your same false casting and at the release point, let go of the line in the line hand. If your timing is right, it will again shoot forward with extra distance.

Now let me tell you a casting secret that is a big help in shooting or releasing the line. To add further control over your line as it is released and shoots forward, form a circle or ring with your thumb and forefinger as you let go of the line on the shoot. This effectively forms an additional large guide that the line will snake through on its forward path. With this method of line/shooting control, the problems of line smashing the stripping guide or wrapping itself over the rod shaft are eliminated.

Hold hands close together when shooting line and form an "O" ring with your thumb and forefinger.

A fun exercise

The final practice session should be lots of fun. Make sure you have plenty of room to practice, so select a park, ball field or parking lot. Use a 50-foot tape measure or substitute to mark off distances of 30, 40, 50, 60 feet and longer increments. Place little flags, cloth or tape to aid with measuring.

Our game is called, of course, "Shooting Line," and it works for both youth and adults. From a start line, put out line and lay it to a mark of 30 or 40 feet. Always practice with a leader where it will force the line to turn over. I'm not a big fan of tying yarn on for an indicator, but go ahead and pretend that it is your Special Killer Fly. Strip out a pile of line to lay at your feet, which will serve as the line you will shoot. Do you think you can add 10 extra feet? How about 20? As you complete the cast, measure it off. Maybe you can have some contests with the neighbor next door.

Learning to shoot line will make you a more competent caster. And with casting exercises and games, becoming a good caster is easier than ever before.

Going for Distance

"What is the big deal about casting for distance?" That is the question I am asked most often about flycasting.

When I am knee-deep in a steelhead stream, fishing in saltwater, or casting in a wind, distance casting is a necessary skill. No, you don't usually need to cast and fish at a 75-foot distance, but you do need all of the timing, shooting and hauling ability that goes into distance casting. Less than 25 percent of all flycasters have the advanced or expert ability to reach this longer mark. The simple explanation for this difficulty is that more mistakes are associated with casting for distance than any other cast.

Distance casting is relative to ability. Beginners need to cast up to 50 feet; intermediates can reach 65 feet; those who are advanced should cast a standard fly line 75 feet; and experts must cast to 85 feet. Most flycasters are also aware that you can achieve a greater distance by using a heavier rod/line. Competitive casters can boom it over 100 feet with a 5-weight rod.

Another trick to get extra distance is to use a shooting-taper fly line. It is commonly 30 feet long followed by a separate running line. A shooting taper puts the most bend in the rod to get extra length on a cast. This line is used most often in steelheading situations.

Common distance mistakes

Overpowering the rod is a typical mistake at all ability levels. A caster tries to attain the magic distance by hammering the rod and forcing the line to extend farther. Tailing loops are one result of this inappropriate application of power. Poor loop formation and timing problems also result. Power does not produce a longer cast, but increased line speed does.

Some flycasters take another dead-end route by making long casting strokes throughout their distance-casting sequence. This leads to some of the same issues as overpowering the rod. A longer cast is usually made up of several false casts that perform the function of gradually lengthening the line. For example, you may make your first false cast with 40 feet of line out. The line is increased by hauling or shooting to lengthen to 50, another false cast to 60, and so forth. You need to use casting strokes to match the various distances (short for a shorter cast, long stroke for longer distance). If someone were to watch your casting sequence, it would proceed from short casting strokes to long.

To make the longest distances, a flycaster must be able to lengthen his casting stroke to the maximum. Lee Wulff, who was well over 6 feet tall, would regularly use a 6-foot bamboo rod for his casting to achieve long casts. With long arms, he was able to swing the rod with a long stroke to reach Atlantic salmon at 70 to 80 feet. If a regular stroke is used that stops at the shoulder, many extra inches of stroke length are lost.

By lifting your rod hand up and behind your shoulder, you get the longest possible stroke. Also, the Lefty Kreh technique of sweeping the rod to the side and rear gives you a very long space to use for your power stroke. Without the additional reach provided by these methods for distance casting, your regular stroke will only produce a typical cast of 50 or 60 feet.

A good formula to use for distance casting is that a tight loop plus high line speed equals your longest distance possible (or the most possible energy needed to cheat a wind). Because it is easy to let your presentation cast drift forward, a tight loop can open up and lose energy. Work hard at making your casting stroke with a smooth application of power that speeds up to a decisive stop. This crisp stopping of the rod forces the rod tip over a small arc and produces a very tight loop.

Practice exercises

If you want to practice or train for longer casts, let me suggest a series of exercises. I prefer practicing on a large lawn area or an open parking lot. To assist with measuring and to provide a straight line, I use a 100-foot Stanley reel-type tape measure. You may want to use cones or stick markers in the ground to mark distance points. Lay out your tape measure and clear your forward and backcasting areas; this can take 150 to 200 feet. Strip off the needed line from your reel and lay it away from your standing position. It is helpful to both clean your line and to pull it between your hands to straighten any small kinks.

Let's start with a distance cast of 50 feet and longer. I call this **"casting the head."** Pull at least 50 feet of line through your guides and lay it straight in front of you. Notice that you have a very short front taper, maybe up to five feet long, that is followed by, in this example, a weight-forward taper. This taper expands for a distance of 30-45 feet, depending on the line manufacturer. On the back end of the weight-forward taper is a much thinner, level running section of line. Take a permanent magic marker and color a black indicator mark around the fly line a couple of feet past the end of the weight-forward taper. With a leader and your "doctored" weight-forward head extended to the front, you can now do some practicing. The black mark should be located at the tip guide. This is an exercise where you will firmly pick up your leader and the 40 or so feet of fly line to your black mark and backcast to the rear. After the line extends properly, power to the front and shoot line from your line hand. Again, false cast to the rear, come to the front, and shoot. This is a good exercise for beginners and intermediates.

Bear demonstrates measuring casting for distance, standing to one side to allow a student (not in picture) to cast squared to the tape measure.

A variation of this practice is good for intermediates. You begin in the same fashion, but instead of doing a simple shoot to the front, perform a **single haul** or pull to the front. Make sure that the haul distance equals the power stroke length and that the haul is timed along with the power stroke. Release the line from your line hand as the loop has formed off the rod tip. This should get you even more distance than a regular shoot.

Distance casting is a perfected skill that will enable you to address many difficult fishing situations. As you work at getting a long line, your entire casting game will improve. After you master this level of distance casting, you can advance to add double hauling to your skills. So what are you waiting for? It's time to practice.

Part Four: Advanced

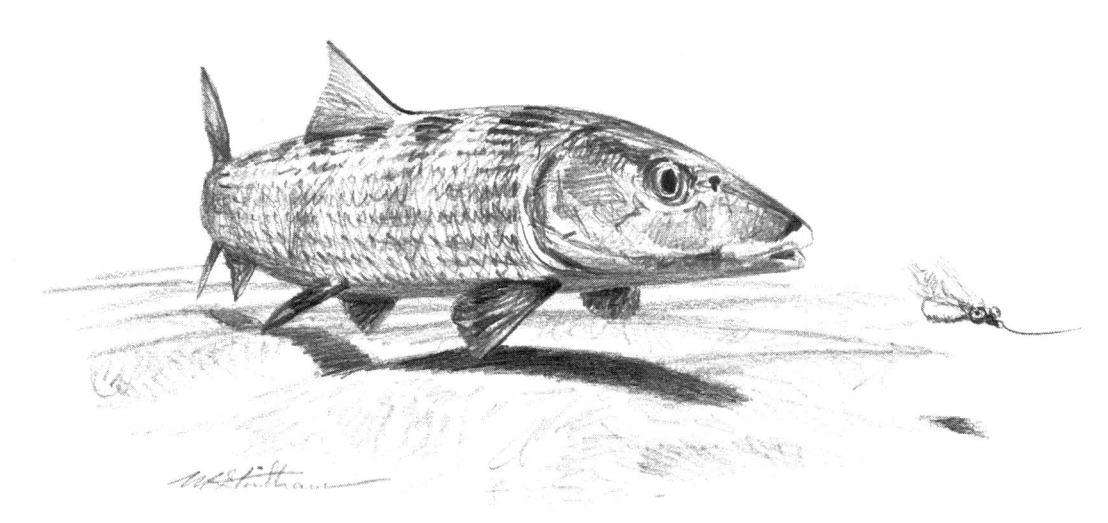

The most difficult effort in flycasting is to make hundreds of casts in a day with a full sinking line in stillwater fishing. This situation requires good flycasting technique, stamina, concentration and a strong casting arm. Like most flyfishers, I'll torture myself any day for the biggest fish. Have you read articles or books by Denny Rickards? He nets dozens of 20-inch trout each year by fishing lakes. An average person may be fortunate to land one or two during that time frame. Sinking lines take you deep and hold your offering in the big fish zone.

Another advanced setting is the pinpoint accuracy that is sometimes needed in fresh or saltwater. On a trip to Christmas Island in the South Pacific, I found myself without a guide nearing my last day. Fishing was spotty, with just enough action to hold your attention. Usually, a bonefish would come into your field of vision at about 40 feet, and your Charlie or Gotcha teased the silver speedster at around 30. For some reason, I happened to notice a large fish come out of deep water to work the edge of the flat about 75 feet away. Patience is a bonefishing virtue, but this fish had grown large in its wariness and I would only get one cast.

With nothing to lose, I pitched the fly in front of the fish by a couple of feet. Not too close. The fish came like a dog on a bone (or maybe a bone on a bone). The fish turned immediately for deep water, was off the shelf and cut me off on coral. Wow! It is exciting even when the trophy fish gets away. Accuracy was the key, and that's something you really master at the advanced level.

Casting Problems with Sinking Lines

Do you realize that over 90 percent of our available water and fish resources are in lakes and seas? So why do 90 percent of our flyfishers only fish in streams? In large lakes, fish can typically be found at depths of 20 feet and more. How can you even present a fly to fish that deep? Most fly guys turn to their spinning gear just to get some action.

At Boca Paila, on Mexico's Yucatan Peninsula, you can enjoy excellent bonefishing on thin-water flats. In the heat of the day or on feeding sprees, the bonefish will head for deeper water of three to five feet to school together and root out tiny crabs and other morsels. Finding these "mudding fish" is quite easy because of the cloudy or milky coloration of the water. A sink-tip or intermediate sink line is necessary to cover these fish. I caught 20 fish in a two-hour period, but casting and controlling the sinking "slime" line was a must.

The best way to approach fish in deeper water is to use a sinking or sink-tip line. These lines are rated in various densities or sink rates (the number of inches the line will sink per second), which the flyfisher matches to the depth of water being fished. If you have tried a sinking line, you know that it casts differently than your smooth floating line.

One of the primary reasons flyfishers stick to rivers is that they have trouble casting sinking versions of line. Our goal for this casting lesson is to let you in on some secrets of successful casting in lake settings and deeper, fast-moving streams. Read Denny Rickards' book about flyfishing lakes and you'll become a convert to sinking techniques.

Difficulties with sinking lines

The problem with sinking lines is very simple: most people can't cast them, or more fairly, don't know how to cast them. With any portion of your line below the surface of the water at depths sometimes over five feet, it is difficult to lift a long length of line to the surface to break it free for the following cast. One of Lefty Kreh's principles of casting applies directly to this: "You cannot make a cast until you get the tip of your line moving." If you try to lift or pick up too much line, the line tip will not move smoothly and freely. Conversely, if you strip in so much line that you can see the leader connection, you've brought the line in too far. Like most things in life, we are seeking balance in the matter.

Let me describe this casting problem in action. My goal is to work a woolly bugger at about 15 feet in depth. I'm casting a Type IV sinking line with a rate of five inches of drop per second. I want to cast 50-60 feet, which allows the line to sink to depth and be fished back. If I work the fly all the way back to my pontoon boat or float tube, I'll begin my next cast with somewhere between five to 10 feet of line out along with my leader. Even for a good caster, it will take six or eight false casts to re-lengthen the line for the next cast. This same situation exists on a trout or salmon river when you strip in too much line. With all of that extra, wasted false casting, we become more tired and catch fewer fish.

The second problem is even worse and stems from trying to make a cast with too much line out. Following the same scenario, if I try to avoid all of the false casting to pick up and begin my cast with 25-30 feet of line, I cannot get the tip of my line moving instantly. Again, it takes a great deal of lifting to get the line to the surface. The line itself might still be at a depth of five feet or more. This means that I cannot start loading and powering my rod until it is almost vertical or directly overhead. To correct this, I continue with my casting motion and throw the line on the water surface behind me. If I am lucky, it doesn't end up in a messy pile that forces an entirely new cast. As I begin my forward cast, I have to rip the line off the water behind me, assuming it hasn't begun to sink and create additional problems.

Solving the problem

My solution involves awareness, timing and technique. The first step in curing your casting ills with a sinking or sink-tip line is to always be aware of how much line you have remaining to begin the next cast. This is important. You can't have too little and you can't have too much. I try to begin my following cast with 15-20 feet of fly line remaining in the water. On a sink-tip,

Deep fish like this nice rainbow trout (caught on Wheat's Lake, in Dillion, Montana) can only be reached with sinking lines.

this is usually the tip plus a little of the floating body. On a full sink line, you can use a white, silver or gold permanent pen to mark the ideal lifting point.

The second secret is to lift all of your line to the surface so you are not fighting water drag and tension. I do this with a **roll cast pick-up** (the same as a regular roll cast, only starting with line underwater). As I lift and position my rod, it pulls the line tip toward me and brings the line closer to the surface. This freely moving line tip signals that I can begin my cast. With a slight pause and stop, I drive my rod forward into a power stroke. The line flies forward and hits the water to the front. That is the timing signal to false cast to the rear. Do not pause and allow the line to sink! When you cast to the rear, perform a single haul (tug or pull) of six to eight inches with your line hand. This breaks any surface tension on the water and shoots your line to the back. In fact, as the line straightens to the rear, open your line hand and your line will lengthen and shoot. Come to the front with a short haul and release, and you have out about 50 or more feet of line. For most fishing situations, this is enough line to fish. This technique of hauling and shooting line will now save you at least half of your false casting.

For longer distances with your sinking lines, add another false cast to the rear and front. This will put you in the 60-feet-plus range. Let me add a comment about line hauling. The haul or pull is made in conjunction with your power stroke. Also, form as tight a loop as possible to avoid throwing your line over into the water to the front or rear. Remember to practice this by sitting on the grass and false casting. This sitting position is almost the same orientation as casting from a float tube or kick boat. Also, practice the feel of a roll cast pick-up with false casting and shooting. This isn't very easy on grass, but you get a much better feel for the technique and become better prepared for the lake.

Another problem with the longer heads on 30-foot sink-tip lines is that they have a tendency to hinge over or drop sharply to the front and rear in false casting. This is typically caused by the entire 30 feet of the sinking portion being out of the rod tip along with five feet or more of the lighter floating/running section. I treat the sinking section like a shooting head. Only allow two or three feet of running line out instead of the longer lengths. Use your best hauling skills to speed the line and release for a long shoot. The heavier sink-tip will pull the running line to a 60- to 70-foot distance, and the line hinge will disappear.

I hope this doesn't sound esoteric or like rocket science. Any beginning or intermediate caster can learn to cast a sinking line with practice. I highly recommend practicing on a pond. Also, when free lessons are being offered at your neighborhood fly shop, ask to use a sinking line. If you are going to pay $50 or more for the latest technology and get a good line, they should show you how to use it. Also, explain where you are going to be fishing and your fishing pros will have suggestions on the proper line. I head to the lake with as many as four different lines in floating and sinking versions to cover the various situations I will face. One way to ease into this sink-line casting is to use either the short 5-foot sink-tip or try an intermediate, slow sink. In the right situations, both of these lines are superb for fish catching.

On Time, On Target: Flycasting Accuracy

Having spent seven of my 27 years of military service in field artillery, I know quite a bit about accuracy. I recall a gunnery contest between the Americans and British that was held at a German training area. We were at an observation post on a ridge overlooking the target area. The Brits fired first and were within 20 yards of the target with shells scattering all about. Countering, the U.S. battery placed their volley exactly on the bull's-eye. With proper austerity the British commander commented, "Nice shooting, chap," to which the American CO replied, "On time, on target."

Bear demonstrates that with advanced skills, good mechanics and aim can be applied even to casting with multiple rods.

The artillery motto of *"on time, on target"* fits flyfishing perfectly. Many times your fly needs to be presented quickly and accurately or you'll never take the fish. In the middle of a blizzard hatch of blue-wing olives on the Provo River, I have seen brown trout only move an inch or two to the side to sip the plentiful naturals. They absolutely refused to move because of all the food in their narrow feeding lane. Accurate upstream casts on the fishes' noses were the only way to entice them.

Think of all the fishing situations that demand a nearly perfect cast. Casting underneath overhanging limbs of mangroves in Florida requires complete control. Placing your hopper against the bank on the Green River can be a study in accuracy. Also, keeping your fly in the feeding lane of rising fish is an exercise in pinpoint presentation. Just how accurate are you? Can you be "on the money" at 20, 30 or 40 feet? What are some of the casting problems associated with accuracy?

Targeting mistakes

One primary flycasting mistake is to direct your fly high above your target on your final presentation cast. As your fly descends, a puff of wind or a slight tug on your rod can cause your fly to miss by feet. To correct this mistake, tilt your casting plane so that you are high on your backcast and low to the water on the front. This also delivers the fly first in front of the leader and fly line.

It is also helpful to engage your line hand when casting for accuracy. As you false cast toward the target, shoot small amounts of line with each false cast to the front. That is a good technique to measure distance and get your fly in the zone. Most people want to go for broke and shoot whatever line is available, with the typical presentation landing way beyond target. Also, don't forget that you can use your line hand to pinch down and stop the forward movement of the line if it is traveling beyond the target. Remember to make a circle with the index finger and thumb of your line hand (practice this as you read) as you release line when shooting to the front. Again, if you are too far, pinch the circle closed.

Another big error in accuracy is not controlling the size of your casting loops. A small, tight loop is highly energized and drives toward your target. Many people suffer from a floppy, loose wrist, which produces large, uncontrollable loops that are very inaccurate. Practice keeping your wrist in a taut and locked posi-

Sighting down your rod and line improves aiming in casting.

tion while casting. Along with a good, even power stroke, which comes to a crisp speed-up and stop, this firm wrist will aid in producing tight loops.

The position of your rod and casting hand are supremely important to accuracy. Just like throwing darts, if you bring your hand and rod in front of your face, you will have better hand/eye coordination. For a cast up to 30 feet, this **in-front-of-your-face position** works well. As casting distance increases, move the rod closely beside your head to allow for a longer casting stroke. People who cast to the side can have real troubles with accuracy. In fact, many side-armers have a tendency to stop their rod a little across their body and produce a curve in their line to the left (if they are right-handed). With the rod extended to the side and away from your eye, it is impossible to sight down your rod (like a gun barrel) to the target.

Advanced flycasters have the extra advantage of hauling (making small pulls or downward jerks) to create more line speed, which turns the fly over to the front and aids in forming tight loops. When you combine hauling with a **hovering technique**, you have the tools for the greatest accuracy. Hovering is a false-casting method that uses extra power to extend your fly over the target and measure proper distance. Do not allow the fly to touch down, but get it close over the water. Keep your casting plane high in the back and low to the front. This multiple false casting near the target can give you the most exact results.

Practice exercises

Practicing for accuracy is one of the fun aspects of flycasting. It doesn't take a great deal of space, so most yards work fine as a practice area. Begin by tying a piece of yarn to the end of a regular 3x, 4x or 5x leader by using a clinch knot. Trim the yarn with scissors so there is little air resistance and bulk. Place children's hula hoops as targets at various distances of 25, 30 and 40 feet. Remember to use a good rod position tight to your face. Angle your casting plane to tilt low in the front. Form good controlled, tight loops, and deliver your yarn fly inside the hoops. As you get better, exchange the hoops for Frisbees or plastic dinner plates.

Another game is to cast as close to the edge of the sidewalk, driveway or road as possible. This simulates casting tight to the bank. Give yourself points if you are within 12 inches, 6 inches, etc. If you hit the driveway, subtract points.

Many fishing situations require casting underneath tree limbs or bank overhangs. Our yard has some spruce and fir trees that are nice to cast under. Try tilting your head in a lowered position and hold your rod in a lowered and matching tilted position. Add some extra power to extend the fly on the turnover to snap underneath the object. If you are treeless, use a folding chair or ottoman as a target. The neighbors won't think this is any odder than casting at hula hoops.

Bear practices hitting a variety of hula hoop targets.

Just two more points about accuracy. The most accurate cast is a typical straight-line cast to the target. In some fishing situations, you must quickly add line mending for the best presentation. Also, don't forget that the fly line and fly will travel in the direction that you speed up and stop the rod. Work on your casting to control your casting arc/stroke so you can deliver your fly most accurately to the side, overhead or backhand.

Getting your fly to the fish is just as important as fly selection. An accurate flycaster is always going to catch more fish than someone just getting it in the general vicinity. Practice your accuracy and you'll find a vast improvement in your flyfishing game.

Hauling for Optimum Line Speed

Along with casting for distance, single and double hauls are critical for line control, accuracy and overcoming wind problems.

Hauling is the downward tug, pull or yank by the line hand in opposition to the power stroke. This pulling apart of the hands places a quick or deep bend in the rod tip, effectively loading the rod. This optimum performance of both hands in flycasting produces optimum line speed.

Single hauling

A **single haul** can be performed to the rear, front or in both directions. Hauling on line pickup helps with breaking water tension and getting the line under control. I call this "getting the line on the rod tip." By hauling, a caster can lift and pick up more line for a cast. The steps for this hauling procedure are to begin at the good starting position of line straight and rod tip low, lift the rod with a loading move, begin your power stroke/move and haul with the same timing and distance. If you were to film this action, you would see the hands stay close together and parallel during the lift and loading move then pull away from each other sharply during the power stroke. As the power stroke comes to a speed-up and stop, the line hand returns close to the rod hand in an "up" position.

The routine problems facing flyfishers are poor timing with the haul and stroke, hauling for a longer distance than the stroke length, and hauling with too much or too little force. Like most casting, a hauling move is smooth and poetic; it looks and feels right.

By releasing line as the power move is completed and the line loop is forming off the rod tip, the line shoots to the rear to add length. Note that you do not have to shoot line on a haul. If you do not release line, the haul still produces a highly energized line and rod with a tight loop for good control and slicing a breeze.

A single haul to the front is helpful in driving a weighted fly or large dry fly forward in presentation, assists to straighten a sinking or sinking-tip line, and aids with a wind to the front. The primary situation in which to use a single haul in both directions

In hauling, the line hand follows the rod hand before the downward pull. No line slack is allowed to form between the line hand and stripping guide.

is when you have a wind coming to your back side. Pick up line with a single haul to the rear and drive and straighten the line with good control by hauling to the front.

Double hauling

The single haul comes from the 1800s, but the double haul was introduced by American tournament caster Marvin Hedges in 1938. Stiffer rods, particularly modern graphite ones, withstand the heavy bending caused by hauling in sequence in both directions. A softer fly rod like the parabolic bamboo or whippy fiberglass models bend so deeply that a double haul still only produces wide, anemic casting loops. My personal preference is to cast with a fast action rod that has a quick tip section. In normal casting, the tip casts a short line with nice loops. For double hauling the rod bends and recovers quickly without wobbling and throwing shock waves into the line.

One of the best ways to get your highest line speed (and to face windy situations, as described later) is to learn the **double haul**. I caution intermediate casters from using the double haul because most do not track their rods in a straight line while casting or have other significant flycasting problems. In that case, the double haul becomes a crutch that is employed to cover other deficiencies from poor casting.

The double haul is seen by the flyfishing world as the pinnacle of achievement in casting skill. As people try to cross this casting hurdle, they find that coordination, timing and hard work are prerequisites. Many books, articles and videos capture the pull, jerk or down/up motion necessary to perform the double haul, and I will not repeat their instruction. Mistakes come from making too long of a pull, really ripping at it. Your pulls should be in synch with your casting stroke and be of the same approximate length. Short strokes mean short pulls. Long strokes mean long pulls. Try this in practice.

A second mistake is to make your downward pull without returning your line hand to a position near your rod hand. This leaves your line hand in the wrong place and either results in awkward, weak pulls or injects killing slack into the cast. Remember: "down/*up*."

Practice exercises

To reach the advanced level of casting 75 feet or to overcome heavy wind, you must double haul. Set up as you did for the "Going for Distance" exercises (see Part 3), and begin with your leader and line to the front. Pick up your line with a single haul to the rear and do not release line into a rearward shoot. Begin your forecast and add a single haul to the front. With this good line speed, release your line into a forward shoot. Before the line loses energy or sags at the front, stop the forward movement of your line by pinching it off with your line hand. Start a second false cast to the rear with a haul and line shoot this time. At maximum load, return to the front for your presentation and final haul. This final haul to the front should generate your best line speed and will be your longest yet. Try to have this last cast stop a little higher than normal so your line can extend to its fullest at the front.

While hauling, apply power appropriately — to the fore- or back-cast, as necessary — to overcome wind.

My favorite double-haul practice is performed by using the long tape measure as a straight-line indicator. Lay out the full 100 feet with your starting position being in the middle and slightly more than one rod length away from the tape. Here you will make your double haul to the side with your line following the path of the tape measure. If you use too much wrist or if you do not stop your rod in a straight line, your casting will fall away from the straight standard. This practice forces you to do the double haul in conjunction with good mechanics.

Begin with 30-40 feet of fly line out of the rod tip and extended to the front and parallel to the tape measure line. First, haul to the rear, stop the rod properly, and shoot line. Do not try to hold the line in the air by false casting, but let it fall to the ground. Is it on line and almost on top of the tape? Did it distance to the rear on your shoot? Now do a forward cast with your line lying on the ground to the back. As you power to the front, haul a matching distance and shoot and release. Is it straight and longer? After you get the feel for hauling to the front and rear with this method, try lifting your cast off the ground and double hauling. Do this with and without shooting. Seek to get the best loops, line speed and timing.

Pushing the envelope

OK, time for the experts. This is a game to demonstrate double hauling without using your rod hand. Right! You cannot use your rod hand to power the rod. Begin with 25-30 feet of line and go into a regular double-hauling sequence. Keep your rod hand as still as possible. You'll find that as you haul quickly the rod will stay loaded with good loops in both directions. It is a nice demonstration that will show off your casting ability.

Double hauling is essential in overcoming wind and reaching your maximum distance. Master double hauling and you may never have to bemoan the one that got away because you just couldn't get your fly to it.

Beating Windy Situations

While drifting the South Fork of the Snake River, we spotted a school of rising trout actively feeding in a back eddy. The best way to approach these hungry targets was to beach the boat and cast about 30 feet to their feeding positions. Fishing had been slim thus far, so we were all eager for action. A couple of large, healthy cutthroats came to net, then the wind jumped on us. I'm talking about a Western howling, before-the-storm wind. Our flycasters became extremely discouraged as the wind shot the flies back into faces or blew them 10 feet off target. Disgusted, one angler returned to the drift boat in utter defeat. How do you win in a situation like that?

I've had the good fortune to travel to saltwater destinations in Florida, Hawaii, Mexico and Christmas Island. Invariably, it seems that the wind blows more in ocean settings than any other. Maybe it is my negative luck, but I have never faced calm, placid conditions. The flats especially present the maxim, "If you can't reach them, you can't catch them." A fellow flyfisher made me stop fishing at Christmas Island to give impromptu lessons on how to drive your Crazy Charlie into a gusting wind.

Sooner or later a howling wind will destroy your fishing day as surely as ominous black thunderheads spewing jagged lightning will. Being the stubborn person that I am, I refuse to let windy conditions win the battle. Learning the proper casting skills to overcome this problem means that you will extend your fishing day and pick up extra distance. Don't pick up the spinning rod, just learn some wind-cheating secrets.

The major difficulties

The number 1 problem with casting in a wind is that casters continue to use a basic overhead cast without adjusting themselves to wind direction. For instance, a strong wind at your casting hand side will blow your backcast behind you and past your opposite side. As you bring the rod forward, the line and fly are aimed at the back of your body. My son Geoff slammed a weighted shad dart into the back of his head like this. It wasn't a pretty sight. I'm sure you have done something similar.

A crisp wind at the front will cause medium to large-size casting loops to collapse, with your line dying in a pile to the front. Bending your wrist during your casting sequence creates especially troublesome, ineffective loops. Also, a high rod position puts the line higher into the wind than a lower delivery.

Winds at your back are sometimes just as troublesome. A normally powered cast results in the line being stopped by the wind and not laying out to the rear, which also does not allow the rod to load properly. Have you ever had the line push back and tangle in the rod? Messy, messy.

The wind direction that causes the fewest problems is one that approaches from your opposite shoulder toward your rod hand. This sweeps the line and fly away from your body and at least permits a somewhat normal cast. But on the saltwater flats, it is sad to see a guide repeatedly repositioning the boat because an ineffective caster can only present a fly from a certain position.

A second major problem that occurs while fishing is that the fly is stripped in too close, which doesn't leave much line out to load the rod. Without a good bend in the rod, it is not able to power the line in these windy situations. The simple fix for this error is to work the fly in until 30-35 feet of line is still out. Following this method, you can get a decent loading for shooting or hauling.

Overcoming windforce

Let's focus on the most basic problem that winds present, no matter which direction they are blowing. Wind creates extra work to overcome during the physics of casting. Extra work demands extra power or line speed. First, apply a double haul to increase line speed and tighten/narrow your loop. It is this driving speed that reduces the effects of the wind. Next, think of applying extra power in the direction that the wind is coming from, such as the front or back. A tailwind begs for a more powerful and longer backstroke with less power to the front, because the cast will sail like a kite with the wind. Aim the backcast low under the wind with a high forecast to carry farther. Facing winds take an easier backcast, with a thrusting, powerful front delivery low to

Geoff models a good off-hand cast for a wind blowing from the caster's rod-hand side.

the water. Winds abate slightly closer to land or water, so put it low. Another cast is to lift a high backcast that stands up in the wind and, by tilting the plane of your cast low in the front, punches a high-energy cast under the wind.

The attacking wind at your casting hand side can discourage anyone. Big hooks zinging close to your ears can put the fear of God into any set of waders. Try using a nonstandard **oval cast** as a remedy. Begin your cast by bringing the rod three-quarters or sidearm to your casting side. When the line extends to the rear, tilt the rod over your head for a backhand return to the front. Your rod movement has essentially scribed an oval that holds the line in tension and always keeps the fly far from your body. It is the safest cast that you can make with this condition. You can also use a backhand/offhand cast that takes the rod, line and fly away from your body on the opposite side. These casts take practice to master, so head for your favorite practice site and work on them.

A wind from your line-hand side directed toward your rod hand is the easiest to overcome. It keeps the line and fly pushed away from your body. Often, you need to add extra power to this cast as well to overcome the effects of the wind and keep your line in control and your fly delivered with accuracy.

Practice exercises

Now for some casting exercises to help develop the skills to tackle nasty winds. It is important to practice under windy conditions. Make sure that you have a large open space like a field, park or parking lot, and work with about 30 feet of line. By turning your body as you practice, the wind will hit your front, back, opposite side and casting-hand side. Try to apply smooth power to your cast with enough to straighten the line. Be careful not to overpower the cast and create wind knots (bad casting knots) in your leader.

The headwind in your face is the most difficult. Lower your body slightly and place your right foot (for right-handers) to the rear, so you can rock back and reach farther to the rear with your casting stroke. First, make a normal cast and check the results. Next, power your false cast more and shoot line on the delivery. Better. Now, double haul (learn this technique!) and add power with a wider stroke. You should be able to bust through the wind with your best cast.

Don't let windy situations keep you from fishing. As you develop your skills and keep practicing, the wind will turn out to be little more than a nuisance.

Part Five: Expert

My son Geoff became the youngest FFF-certified casting instructor at age 15 and also represented the United States as a member of Team USA at the 1999 World Youth Flyfishing Championships in Ireland. Now, at 19, he regularly works as a flyfishing guide to pay his college expenses as he prepares to become an Air Force officer. I vividly recall that as a second-grader in Germany, Geoff would watch the Mel Krieger casting video over and over. Even early on, he had the physical and mental skills to become a professional.

Flyfishing holds many intangibles and variables for all of us. If we approach the game casually and infrequently, we achieve mediocre results. Certainly the converse is true as well; that if we give flycasting our maximum effort by practicing, taking lessons, physically strengthening ourselves and learning from others, we can become an expert. There is another personal characteristic that is critical for those who would reach the top of their game: There must be a fire burning within. I can spot it in people and I like to "stoke the flames." Sometimes I'm a cheerleader, other times a hard-nosed coach.

Like so many others prizes in life, we don't reach the pinnacle without having sacrificed the time, effort and money to become the best that we could be. Let me tell you a small secret. The overall best flycasters in the world are from Europe.. Many learned casting as a sport in school, but the number one reason is that they have more of a passion and desire. This drivenness is daunting, yet exemplary. As my father used to say, "Deciding what you want to be is half the journey in getting there."

The "S" cast produces a series of waves in the line that assist in drag-free presentation.

Presentation Casts

Presenting the fly is a current hot topic in flyfishing circles. Many books are addressing the subject, though, in actuality, it is not new but has always held a center stage for fishers.

One anchor premise in presentation is making the required cast and mends. Presentation casts are made by manipulating the fly rod by tilting the casting plane, hand movement, and stopping the rod. There are numerous presentation casts that are sometimes delivered in tandem. Most are used to throw slack into the line as it lands upon the water so stream currents will pull on this extra line and allow a drag-free float. Some are also used to drive a nymph or streamer into the water first and get maximum depth. Learning a variety of presentation casts to accompany regular straight-line methods adds to the flyfisher's arsenal of fish-catching techniques. From beginners to experts, the fisher that gains mastery in presentation will always land the most difficult fish.

Types of presentation

Let's begin with an "**S**," **snake** or **wiggle cast**. In a stream situation that has fish holding in slower water or a pocket beyond the main current, an "S" cast is a good choice to give your fly a good drift. With rising trout and when making upstream casts, this wiggle of line on slight or moderately swift water gives the very best natural float. It is best to use a longer leader with this technique, so that only the leader will pass over the feeding fish.

Practicing the **"S" cast** is relatively easy and is a good foundation for other presentation casts. You don't need much space; the front yard works alright. Begin with 25 feet of line lying straight in front of you. Use some energy and move or wiggle your rod hand horizontally. The result is a series of waves. Next, make a normal straight-line, overhead cast. As the line forms a loop and comes off your rod tip, begin this same horizontal hand movement. Your hand is pushing the tip from side to side and the line follows the rod tip. For additional practice, wait longer into the delivery cast before you begin your shake. This places your wavy squiggles more into the middle of the line. Try moving your hand just a little, then with a broader motion. Narrow motion produces a tight "S," broad motion a wide pattern.

The **puddle**, **pile** and **parachute casts** are all variations of the same theme with different instructors using the names somewhat interchangeably. Placing your forward cast so that the main body of the fly line lands in a pile with little S curves is your objective. Some poor casters do this almost instinctively by casting to the front in huge open loops and driving their rod toward the water in the front. The line energy doesn't let the fly line straighten and it collapses.

To get a good piling cast, tilt your final backcast low to the rear and aim over head-high to the front. When your straight-line cast is fully extended in the front, lower your rod (which was still pointed skyward) at a quicker speed than gravity would make the line fall. If you watch closely, the body of the line will hit the water first and the leader and fly will land gently last. An experienced caster can also lower the rod later in the delivery and place the pile of slack closer to the angler over a near current.

Lowering the rod quickly after the line has extended fully causes it to collapse into a puddle cast for drag-free drifts.

For practice, adjust your casting stroke by making a low backcast and a high forecast on a tilted plane. Make several false casts at this high climbing angle. Take care in the rear not to hit the ground, so look over your shoulder till you are comfortable. Fly shop owners like this cast because a lot of flies are lost to grass or brush. It is best over open water like an upstream cast. Once you have grooved this angled cast, drop your rod tip vertically after your line has fully extended. The result should be a nice puddle.

One of my favorite casting styles, which I learned in Germany, is the oval cast, and it works very well with these parachuting casts. An oval cast is brought to the side on the backcast and overhead to the front, with the rod tip making an oval path. It is simple to drop a low backcast and then aim at various heights as you come to the front on a new plane. Try this oval/pile combination and see if you don't get the best results.

Positive and **negative curve casts** are perfect for placing your fly behind obstructions. On the boulder-strewn Madison River, a curve cast can tuck your fly into the holding pocket above or behind exposed rocks. Again, the secret of *all* presentation casts is that the fly line will follow the direction in which the rod tip moves or stops. For the positive or left curve, for right-hand casters, your best casting motion is to come three-quarters to sidearm. Practice this off-overhead stroke and present your yarn fly straight to the front. Now come to the front with a little extra power and stop your rod hard. The line kicks distinctly into a left curve as your rod tip is thrown in that direction. Many right-handed flycasters have a natural curve to the left because of delivering the fly in this manner. Place some Frisbees or plates on the lawn as targets at different ranges. Try to make your left curve cast snap behind these pretend rocks and protuberances.

Presenting the negative or right curve cast is a bit more challenging and takes more practice to become accurate. This is an underpowered cast that is made with a slight hand movement from right to left on the horizontal plane. The trick is to cast the right length of line to the target area and have your line "die" upon the water at the proper moment.

Practice begins again with regular false casting to the front. On your presentation, ease off on your stroke, bring your line in low, and sweep your rod from right to left as your loop is forming off the rod tip. This right-to-left hand movement is painting or scribing the movement of the line. As you aim at your targets, try to drop your yarn fly right over them. An advantage of this right curve is that it lands softly, but it is nearly impossible to use in a wind.

Reach and tuck casts

You can spend hours working on presentation casts, and the **reach cast** popularized by Doug Swisher should be a standard. Once you learn this cast, you will never fear regular currents. The reach cast is essential because you can use it with any type of fly; dry, nymph or streamer.

In the yard, begin with a normal false casting sequence. On the last delivery, let the line straighten and send your yarn fly to the target, then reach your rod to the right or left. This creates a triangle leg over any type of current, with your fly presented accurately. Do some measurements. By reaching your 3-foot arm and 9-foot rod on an angle, you can place about five feet of line into the current. Now the fly can either float naturally or sink to depth.

An important variation is the **reach curve cast**. This cast is made with the right or left reach made during the middle of the cast followed by the rod being pulled to the start position in front. This scribing motion moves the line in a large curve that is an aerialized mend. Once on a bet with my brother, I threw a large reach curve cast with an elk-hair caddis on the tumbling Pit River in California to a steadily rising rainbow. The impossible cast over nasty current produced a fat 17-inch fish and a free dinner for the evening!

Nymphing often requires a deep fly presentation. Getting your weighted fly into the water ahead of a dragging line can be critical, and a **tuck cast** does it best. This cast is delivered with a slightly higher backcast and lower forecast that you will recognize as the opposite of a piling cast. With an overhead, straight-line cast and a distinct stop at the front, your rod tip turns downward and tucks your fly into the water before the line lands.

For practice, tilt the false cast to higher back/lower front. On the last delivery, push your power stroke to a full stop. Your thumb plays an important role in pushing the rod tip over. Push the thumb over at the end of the stroke. Take care in actual fishing to open your loop a bit and keep the fly away from your rod. When you combine the tuck cast with mending, deep, drag-free nymphing can get the fly to large, bottom-holding fish.

When it comes to flycasting and fishing, presentation casts are indispensable. They are a flyfisher's first defense against the real world problems of current, drag and finicky fish. Becoming an expert flyfisher means more than having excellent equipment and fishing regularly: It also means learning to fit your casting presentations to any conceivable situation.

Saltwater Mastery

Over the past 20 years, saltwater flyfishing has provided more new destinations and challenges than any other area of the sport, and there are two specialty magazines dedicated to this exciting game. No wonder many of our fly anglers within driving range of any coast have added bluewater denizens to their quarry list. It is almost comical to hear our land-locked fly club friends admit that they have "bonefish fever." For any flyfisher who has tasted salt, the pull of a 10-pound redfish, 5-pound bonefish, or striper of 25 drives a person to addiction. With this fabulous fishing comes the inherent demand to match your casting to the situation. As I have stated before elsewhere, I believe that saltwater flyfishing has produced more expert casters than any other type.

Let's begin our saltwater adventure close to home and use Florida as our example. Because of business, friends or pleasure, numerous flyflingers make Florida a destination. For saltwater, you can either wade fish or hire a boat. Let's pretend that we are casting for redfish from the bow of the flats boat of my friend, Jon Cave. The foredeck that you stand on should be cleared of obstructions and the boat cleats should be covered by a jacket or carpet. Your line will catch on almost anything. When retrieving line, place it on the deck at your feet. Use care not to step in this pile of line, which is easy to do and spoils any cast.

You would think that in a big ocean, fish aren't that spooky. But no matter their size, fish fit somewhere on the food chain. Wariness is a survival trait. This is sight fishing, and a good saltwater cast is quick, accurate and uses a minimum of false casts. Most casts are thrown in a wind and many must distance as far as 60-70 feet. This is not the stuff of your local bass pond or favorite trout stream.

Using the speed cast

The one cast that is used most often from a boat to meet saltwater prerequisites is the **speed cast**. Begin with line in coils at your feet with the line at the bottom being the last that will shoot from your rod. About 15 feet of fly line is extended from your rod

Bear stands at the ready in a good starting position for the speed cast.

tip with the leader butt junction pinched between your line hand's thumb and forefinger. Also squeezed with this finger combo is the fly. This is called the ready position; in it you are poised to strike at a target fish. You may hold this position for as long as 20 or 30 minutes waiting for the payoff. If you spot a fish or the poler gives you direction and distance, forcefully throw your fly, leader and line away from the boat. You will rarely get this line to fully extend, but snap it into a powered backcast and slip some line to the rear if you are able. Come to the front with a haul and shoot, lengthening your line to around 35 feet; haul and shoot to the rear to 50 feet; then make your final delivery with a haul and shoot to 70 feet. If you have any extra false casting, you are either wasting false casts or suffering from poor casting skills.

When it comes time to practice for your trip, use a piece of cardboard or plywood to simulate the boat deck. This gets you in the habit of correct line stacking and assuming the ready position. I like to pretend that I am an osprey readying for action. Follow the previous steps till your speed casting comes easy. Be your worst critic and practice in a wind, too.

There is another start position, which is used when the boat is poled and moving. In this case, I merely let the fly and line drag beside the boat. If a fish is spotted, I complete the rest of the speed cast.

Wading

Another situation in saltwater flyfishing comes in a wading environment, whether it is shore fishing at Cape Cod or flats fishing in the tropics. One handy tool for wading in breakers is a stripping basket. They come in a variety of forms from mesh to hard plastic. A basket stores stripped line between casts and keeps it from tangling for following casts. After having a guide step on my line and almost sever it at Christmas Island, I appreciate a basket keeping the line away from my feet and from dragging uncontrollably in the surf.

A helpful technique is to use proper stripping and to loop your incoming line in your line hand in preparation for the next cast or changing positions. On the flats, a typical strip is six to 12 inches. Upon making three or four strips, make a large loop and hold it over your last three fingers. Keep making these large loops until you are prepared to recast. Store and carry the line with this large loop method if you are sight fishing and stalking fish. As you are wading, clinch the fly with your thumb and forefinger in the speed cast fashion. With this method, you can get your fly over a bonefish in seconds.

Always be aware of the wind direction while wading. This is easily done by throwing out a cast and observing how the wind blows your line. If you have to hit a head breeze, try to single haul and slip as much line to the rear as possible, which gets you a maximum load for a forward cast and haul. Keep the flyfishing guide away from your casting hand side and reposition him if you need to come to your backhand for casting. Because a guide is so focused on locating and spotting fish, he is often stationed right where your line needs to be.

Many flyfishers progress on their pilgrimage from just catching fish, to catching lots of fish, to catching the biggest fish.

Bluewater angling gets a flyfisher to the largest fish possible. Tuna, wahoo, sailfish, dorado and marlin are all possible on the long rod. If you are going to the back alley to fight one of these brutes, you must be in good physical shape to handle the hot climates and aggressive, large fish. Long casts are not as important as quick, accurate casts to teased or chummed fish. Practice your casting with the heavy outfit that you must use to withstand this battering. Many of the lifting rods for tuna and marlin run from 13- to 18-weights! When you add a large bluewater fly reel, an outfit can weigh three times the amount used for small trout. Fortunately, a flycaster does not have to make cast after cast, but only as a fish shows.

A favorite line for most bluewater species is a full sinking or long, 30-foot sink-tip line. These lines are the most difficult to load of any in flyfishing. Because these rods are so large and stiff for lifting, it is a challenge

A stripping basket is an excellent tool for holding line and keeping it away from rocks and obstructions.

Stripping line in and forming loops to prepare for the next cast while wading.

to get the line to bend the rod. They are also a pain to roll cast. If you practice with your actual outfit, you will be familiar with the demands of this macro environment.

Bluewater means off-shore, so your casting is from a 30- to 50-foot cruiser or 25- 30-foot center console sportfisher. On a trip to the Big Island of Hawaii, I flyfished with Del Decker, a bluewater specialist, on the *Reel Action*. He has four primary techniques for getting a person into fish. With little or no experience, you can troll a fly at the surface. This works like regular teaser plugs and gets plenty of hookups while covering lots of water. Chumming is a good choice when you are in a likely fish holding area. When the fish are at or near the surface, cast your fly and let it sink like a dead or injured baitfish. Del's low-sided boat allows a flyfisher to cast from the front or rear without outrigger poles and lines to block a good presentation.

Teasing brings the angry fish near the boat where you can get in a cast. As the fish comes close, the teaser is pulled from the water and replaced by any accurately cast fly. Flies can be tandem rigs often 8 to 10 inches long, so prepare yourself for a clumsy

The ready position at the front of the boat in bluewater fishing. If fish appear, the rod can be quickly in hand.

feel. The buddy system is an exciting way to get multiple hookups. Regular trolling gear is employed to hook the first fish, which, hopefully, is traveling in a bunch. As the tuna or dorado is worked to the boat, be prepared to launch your cast to its "buddy" or another fish following the hooked fish. This is both fun and mayhem. Once, a group of us had four bonito on at once.

Flyfishing from a cruiser presents the inherent problems of being higher off the water and the obstructions of the boat's cabin and outriggers. For an IGFA catch, the boat must be pulled out of gear and a regular flycast made. Looking to the rear of the boat, the right stern is the number one position with left stern being secondary. A caster can get a clearer backcast and angle his shot to intersect the teased fish as it is moving into the boat.

Saltwater flyfishing and flycasting are exciting extensions and expansions of a person's abilities. To achieve saltwater mastery takes countless days on water, good guiding and coaching, and a perfection of casting skills. Big fish are a positive affirmation and reward for improving one's game.

Becoming a Certified Casting Instructor

Since 1992, the Federation of Fly Fishers has offered a Casting Instructor Certification Program for the purpose of standardizing flycasting instruction around the world. Overall, the program enhances instruction by increasing instructor knowledge, teaching skills and casting ability. Hundreds of instructors have completed this vigorous program, which has spread across the globe. Instructors are qualified to teach individuals, classes and seminars. You'll find many of these certified people working at fly shops and as guides. But simply becoming a better flycaster has been the primary aim of many people seeking certification. The standards and qualifications to become an instructor are very high and meeting the standard results in improved skills.

There are two levels of certification: basic and master. The master certification builds on the basic program and adds increased skills and an extremely broad knowledge of flycasting, which is tested in a challenging oral examination. As instructors, masters teach in the same venues as basic instructors with the addition of teaching people to become basic instructors and testing candidates at the basic level.

Both men and women are seeking certification and meeting the requirements. At age 15 my son Geoff was the youngest basic certified instructor in America. Becoming a casting instructor demands a dedicated effort from anyone wanting to reach that high mark. What does it really take to pass the test, and how does a person best prepare?

Preparing for the test

The first area to work on is casting skills. Start out with the basics. If you have a problem forming good casting loops, have a floppy wrist, or don't apply power properly, you need to fix these major areas. You should perfect your pick-up and lay-down cast, roll cast and false cast, and shooting line. With coaching or assistance, double hauling should come smoothly and naturally. Another casting skill is accuracy. Practice is essential, so lots of yard time will produce better results. Do not think or assume that you will practice while fishing. Because the focus is on fly selec-

Three highly recommended choices for flyfishing reading. See "Suggested Reading and Viewing" for more information on these and other titles.

tion, reading water and other fishing points, casting is put on the back burner. Try to hone your casting in true practice sessions with the end result being better skills at streamside. Think of flycasting like golf. The driving range, putting and chipping greens are a necessity to the real game.

I hear more complaints over having to meet the distance-casting requirement of 75 feet than any other. One candidate moaned, "Why do we have to cast that far? I never cast that far in a fishing situation." That may be true, but distance casting is a combination of hauling, line speed, and good rod and loop control. You can't hide any weaknesses when it comes to hitting the long one. If you are having trouble with distance, take the necessary lessons to smooth out that part of your game.

The written exam

The comprehensive written exam about flycasting is as difficult as many college finals. Do I have your attention? I have never known a person to pass this test "cold turkey" without having studied. In fact, it is not uncommon to have people miss up to 50 percent of the test questions. Again, complaints run rampant: "These are trick questions!," "No one could pass this test!," "Who made up these questions, some crazy flyfisher?"

By and large, experienced flycasters think they know more about flycasting than they really do. Let me invent a question similar to those you might see on your exam:

"What is the most important cast for beginners to learn?" a) false cast, b) pick-up and lay-down cast, c) reach cast, d) all of the above, e) none of the above.

Is that your final answer? The correct response is "b."

OK, let me share the secret for passing the written portion of the basic casting instructor certification exam. Study the current books and videos about flycasting. You can't go wrong if you select those by Joan Wulff, Mel Krieger and Lefty Kreh. Pay close attention to definitions, e.g., in false casting, your casting loop should extend to the front and rear forming a "J" or candy cane laying on its side. You can use your highlighter to make some of these key points already marked here by **boldface type** further stand out for even easier reference. When you have finished studying, study some more. Just put your books down for a week or two, then begin again until the material becomes ingrained.

Learn to teach by teaching

The final critical section of the test is instructing ability. Some people pass the written and performance areas only to succumb in the teaching skills arena. The best way to learn to instruct is to learn from an instructor (remember the videos) and to teach others. I spent many years teaching youth groups and clubs, which served as a foundation for my certified instructor skills. There are limitless young people who would love to receive free casting instruction. Within five minutes, testing officials will determine if a candidate has experience in teaching. You cannot get a waiver for this third test area; you must be able to instruct.

As you begin teaching, seek to explain casting methodology in the briefest fashion. Long-winded explanations regularly have "bull" stamped upon them. Demonstrate with a rod and also in pantomime your cast or casting error. Many people learn quickly from visual instruction. Make sure that your students are also learning the feel of proper casting. This can even require that you hold the student's hand and make the cast with them.

Certification testing is held at various sites around the country, especially during flyfishing shows and conclaves. Program fees are $50 for testing, $50 for enrollment if you pass, and $25 for yearly certification renewal. Candidates are required to be current members of the Federation of Fly Fishers as well. The FFF can provide additional program information at (406) 585-7592.

Becoming a certified casting instructor is not a goal for everyone, but the program is challenging and produces some of America's best casters. If you think you have the right casting stuff, start working toward certification today.

Sharpening the Mental Game of Flycasting

I am not a sports psychologist and don't claim to be, but I have found a common denominator among all expert flycasters, whether men or women: they are at the top of their mental game.

Without passion, why bother flycasting? I admire Mel Krieger for bringing such infectious passion to casting and instruction.

One of the primary reasons that people get "hooked" on flyfishing is that it is such a challenging mental game. If you flip back your pages of memory, you will find images of days on stream that were a study in detective work. Which fly do I use? Where is the likely holding water? What cast do I make? It doesn't take me long to realize that most of my outings are like that, whether on the river, on the lake or on saltwater. Focus, concentration and the ability to make associations and solve puzzles all contribute to the development of a skilled flyfisher.

All of this is a growth process. You do not suddenly arrive on the scene as an expert. We have all witnessed talented people pick up a fly rod and instantly showcase intermediate ability. Maybe this person is a natural athlete or has transferred a similar skill set from golf or tennis. Did you know that Tiger Woods is a flyfisher? Mark O'Meara, his PGA golfing friend, introduced him to flyfishing, and they pursue their interest on many of our local Utah waters. Does Tiger catch fish? Yes. Is he an expert caster? No. I can beat him any day. No brag, just fact. Even Tiger will concede that time and development go into excellent flyfishing, as with golf.

Long ago in a distant sociology class, I had to write a term paper about whether leaders are born or made. Being the consummate diplomat, I answered "both." Great flycasters are born with natural mental and physical ability, and the sport of flyfishing just seems to fit them. Why are so many of the flyfishing professionals so multi-talented, with such broad-ranging skills? They are renaissance people. They have also sharpened their mental game to make themselves into premier casters. I would like to present some of the mental aspects that must be honed just as much as the physical attributes that go into flycasting.

Reading up

How do you sharpen your mental game? As a youngster, I absorbed books. Besides my catcher's mitt, my favorite possession was my library card. My goal was to read a hundred books every summer. This hunger for information and knowledge is a key to better flycasting. I read and study everything that I can about flycasting. There are numerous books on the market that explain the ins and outs of casting. Even the seemingly antiquated tomes of the past are fascinating. What techniques were used to cast a greenheart rod 200 years ago? You will even find chapters about flycasting hidden in general works about flyfishing. When I want to compare my ideas with Cathy Beck, I just turn to her book.

I have been known to read every magazine about flyfishing on the newsstand as well. You do not always find flycasting columns, but many technique articles will discuss the necessary casts for different situations. My files are filled with articles I have saved for over 20 years.

Using video

In the mid-1980s, instructional videos became a popular means of learning flycasting. The "Scientific Anglers" series featuring Doug Swisher is a classic and standard; there are many others from excellent instructors (see my list of suggested videotapes for more ideas). In the future, I'll offer tips that you can watch on your computer — video delivered via the Internet from AmazingOutdoors.com.

Keep in mind: When you are viewing a video, you are actually taking a lesson. Pay close attention to the instructional style and techniques that you are viewing. With a video source, you are building a stronger mental image of what good flycasting is about. Again, build your knowledge base.

Experts are also naturally teachers; you are learning to teach. There is nothing that ingrains your knowledge quite so much as you yourself instructing. Having to transmit knowledge that produces improved casting skills in others demands your own studied efforts and improvement.

Some top-recommended videos (see "Suggested Reading and Viewing" for more information on these and others).

Envisioning the cast

Many coaches work with their players to image or visualize their best performance. Imaging requires an inward focus that allows you to run your tape of a perfected skill. My sons, freestyle skiers and aerialists, find it impossible to perform without imaging.

Many of us recall those pregame moments of "getting your mind on the game." My difficulty was that I always seemed to float off to Beaver Lake, White River and rainbow trout. I closed my eyes to see leaping bass rather than touchdowns.

Let's go over the ingredients of good flycasting. The sight or visual element of flycasting is critical. Flycasting instructors demand students "do it my way" so the learner focuses on the visual picture of proper casting. My suggestion is for casters to copy the professional flycaster's style that most resembles their own. Flycasting books contain loads of photos that embody the proverbial picture speaking a thousand words. Can you close your eyes and do an out-of-body experience to view yourself casting? You should.

As an exercise, sit in a comfortable chair and envision yourself performing various casts; pick-up and lay-down, roll cast, shooting line, double haul. You can't get there unless you can picture it. I know that you can do this because we do it so often with flyfishing itself. In my own journey, I have countlessly revisited a large, leaping brown trout that escaped 20 years ago. This image is burned into my psyche, representing one more fish to catch, one more river to cross.

There is also a verbal or auditory element to casting. You receive instruction on how to make a cast. In the past flyfishers heard "ten to two" as if casting by a clock face. My hammering instruction is "line straight, rod tip low." It must live as a mantra in some people's heads. For practice, close your eyes and merely listen to the fly line as you false cast. What does it sound like? An almost perfect, rhythmic swish. In stark contrast is a poorly timed cast, which cracks a whip. In your mind, you should hear a swish-swish timed like a metronome.

Feeling the cast, the kinesthetic element, is also critical. The most important feel in flycasting is learning the speed-up and stop of the power stroke. That is the reason I have people practice casting in the car. Again, only do this at a stoplight. Feel the distinct stop at the front; speed up to a stop at the back. Feel the longer stroke and timing of a longer cast. Also, do you ever consider your breathing? Controlled breathing is a wonderful relaxation exercise. Try to mentally "feel" your good casting with this measured breathing.

The final step of perfecting your mental game is to analyze the steps or elements of your casting. Are your hands too far apart? On the double haul, does your line hand make a following upward movement and return to the rod? This is like taking a mental test. Explain to yourself the causes of tailing loops. Most people who fail the instructional section of flycasting certification do so because they have not done this mental analysis for themselves.

Take time to reflect

As a pastor, I tout the benefits of prayer, meditation and reflection. Built into the river of life is a seam or thread that begs us to slow down and calm ourselves. Flyfishing's magic is that it draws people as a peaceful, pastoral endeavor. Many are religiously passionate about flyfishing because it gives them a window for viewing the world as a clean and beautiful place of harmony and order. We step into this perfectly created world momentarily and leave with the powerful desire to return again. I tell audiences that God invented flyfishing because of this beauty and order. As I step from my pulpit back into the stream, do not forget the importance of reflection.

Anyone can sharpen their mental skills in flycasting. It takes work, time and desire. If your personal goal is moving to expert status, perfect your mental game. Tiger has — at least in golf.

Last Cast: Close

Maybe you have noticed it on a dark starry night. Known popularly as Orion, this constellation is easily recognizable. The ancient Greeks also called him "the hunter" as they imagined him with a bow. There is a singular account of a Greek sportsman fishing with a fly; I think it unfortunate they could not envision that web of stars as a flycaster in the middle of a double haul.

Flyfishing does that to you. It gives you a new way of viewing life. Flycasting, of itself, can change your outlook on the world by linking your timing and rhythm to the flow of the stream or the push of the ocean wave. You are drawn into the moment, removed from normal circumstance and become lost in your environment. I believe flycasting is the spiritual heartbeat, the soul, of one's passion for flyfishing.

The art of flyfishing is founded upon the fine art of flycasting. We have joined together to put in our best efforts to understand and improve our casting. "30 Days to Better Flycasting" is not meant to be a cute title, but is intended to communicate that if a casters will actually practice and train for 30 days, they will improve to another skill level or experience positive results. Bear's Casting Aid is a product to assist with good form and technique and never to be a crutch. When you progress beyond it, pass it on to a friend.

As much as anything, our flyfishing should be filled with more fun and less frustration. Worrying about a cast or your ability to perform adequately only plants a self-imposed cloud over your head. Stay within yourself. Maybe casting 100 feet was never in your cards, but placing a fly accurately at 10 yards will garner huge success in many situations. When anger and stress taint our flyfishing, it is time to list our equipment on e-Bay.

Another point for our Last Cast together: Help someone else with their flycasting and flyfishing. Give free lessons to neighborhood kids. Spend time mentoring a beginner. Teaching and studying are the best ways for anyone to gain knowledge and skills and have them imprinted on the fishing psyche. I appreciate all of the people who have helped me on my flyfishing journey and I feel a real obligation to share with others.

Continue to make flycasting a priority in your flyfishing life. Good flycasting will bring you satisfaction and fulfillment along with bigger and better fish. Good casting!

Suggested Reading and Viewing

Books

Beck, Barry and Cathy. *Fly-Fishing the Flats.* Mechanicsburg, PA: Stackpole Books, 1999.

Borger, Gary. *Presentation.* Wausau, WI: Tomorrow River Press, 1995.

Deck, Tom. *The Orvis Streamside Guide to Fly Casting.* New York: The Lyons Press, 2000.

Jaworowski, Ed. *The Cast.* Mechanicsburg, PA: Stackpole Books, 1992.

Jaworowski, Ed. *Troubleshooting the Cast.* Mechanicsburg, PA: Stackpole Books, 1999.

Kreh, Lefty. *Longer Fly Casting.* New York: Lyons & Burford, 1991.

Kreh, Lefty. *Lefty Kreh's Modern Fly Casting Method.* Birmingham, AL: Odysseus Editions, 1991.

Kreh, Lefty. *Solving Fly Casting Problems.* New York: Lyons & Burford, 2000.

Krieger, Mel. *The Essence of Flycasting.* San Francisco: Club Pacific, 1987.

Lord, Macauley. *L.L. Bean Fly Casting Handbook.* New York: The Lyons Press, 2000.

Wulff, Joan. *Joan Wulff's Fly Casting Accuracy.* New York: The Lyons Press, 1997.

Wulff, Joan. *Joan Wulff's Fly Casting Techniques.* New York: The Lyons Press, 1987.

Videotapes

Borger, Gary. *15 Most Common Casting Errors*. Tomorrow River Press/Federation of Fly Fishers, 1996. 13 mins.

Fernandez, Chico. *The Art of Advanced Fly Casting*. Scientific Anglers. 45 mins.

Kreh, Lefty. *Fly Casting with Lefty Kreh*. Tomorrow River Press, 1992. 45 mins.

Krieger, Mel. *The Essence of Flycasting I*. Krieger Enterpises, 1985. 60 mins.

Krieger, Mel. *The Essence of Flycasting II*. Krieger Enterpises. 60 mins.

Swisher, Doug. *Advanced Fly Casting*. Scientific Anglers. 68 mins.

Swisher, Doug. *Basic Fly Casting*. Scientific Anglers. 62 mins.

Wulff, Joan. *Joan Wulff's Dynamics of Fly Casting*. Miracle Productions, Down East Books, 1990. 90 mins.

INDEX

Accuracy   24, 26, 27, 30, 32, 34, 47, 54, 68, 69, 83, 84, **89-93**, 94, 102, 108-110, 113, 114, 116
Advanced skills   23, **25-26**, 27, 55, 67, 73, 79, 83, 84, 91, 96
Basic (pick-up/lay-down) casting   24, **29**, 37
Bear's Casting Aid   **19-22**, 31, 34, 38, 56,
Beck, Barry and Cathy   26, 121
Beginner skills   21, **24-25**, 28, 30, **45-60**
Body positioning   35, 47, **51-54**, 64, 91, 102
Borger, Gary   6, 26, 48
Cave, Jon   110
Certified casting instruction   23, 25, 27, 68, **116-119**, 123
Combination (thumb and forefinger) grip   48
Curve casting   27, **107-108**, 109
Decker, Del   114
Distance casting   38, 64, 67, 68, 72, **75**, 76, 77, **79-82**
Doing the 180   **70-71**
Double haul   **95-98**, 100, 102
Drag-free presentation   87, 105, 109
Eggsercizer   **42-44**
Elbow position   52, **53-54**
Equipment
    for children   **28-29**, 31, 32
    for seniors   **37-38**, 41
    for women   **33-34**
    general   25, 52, 61, 74, 109
Expert skills   64, 79, 98, **103-124**
False casting   20, 60, 69, 70, 75, 76, 77, 78, 81, 86, 87, 88, 91, 92, 96, 97, 102, 107, 108, 109, 110, 111, 116, 118, 123
Federation of Fly Fishers   **6**, 23, 25, 27, 103, **116**, **119**
Floppy wrist   **55-57**, 70, 90, 116
Flycasting ability levels   **23-27**
Forefinger (index) grip   47
Hand-strengthening exercises   **42-44**
Hovering technique   69, 91

Imaging   **120-123**
In-front-of-your-face position   91
Index (forefinger) grip   47
Intermediate skills   21, **61-82**, 88, 95
Jacklin, Bob   6
Kreh, Lefty   6, 73, 80, 85, 118
Krieger, Mel   6, **18**, **31**, 118, 120
Line control   **68-71**, 77, 85, 90, **94-95**, 102, 112
Line hand   **75-77**, 82, 87, 90, 94, 111, 112, 123,
Line speed   **79-80**, 91, **94-98**, 100, 117
Loading   28, 31, 64, 73, 75, 86, **94-96**, 100, 112, 113
Lob cast   **39-40**
Loops   **20-21**, 47, **55-57**, 58, **64-66**, **68-74**, 75, 76, 79, 80, 82, 88, **90-92**, 95, 96, 100, 106, 109, 116, 118, 123
Malone, Karl   51
Mending   92, 105, 109
Nonloop   68
Open loop   **68**, **71**, 106
Overpowering the rod   33, 73, 79, 102,
Pantomime   44, 48, 66, 119
Pick-up/lay-down (basic) casting   24, **29**, 37
Pile cast   106, 107
Pontoon craft   **71**, 86
Power stroke   48, 64, 66, 70, **72-74**, 75, **79-82**, 86-88, 90, 92, 94, 97, 98, 100-102, 107, 111, 116, 123
Practice exercises   44, 69. 70, 71, 76, 77, 80-81, 96, 122
Presentation casts   80, 85, 89, 90, 92, **105-109**, 114
Puddle cast   **106-107**
Rajeff, Steve   6, 26
Reach cast   **108-109**
Richards, Bruce   6
Rickards, Denny   83, 85
Rod grip   28, 33, 34, 38,
Rod hand   64, 76, 80, 94, 96, 98, 100, 102
Rod tip   20, 64, **65**, 68, 70, 73, 74, **76**, 82

INDEX

Roll casts   **63-67**, 87
Roll cast pick-up   88
"S" (snake, wiggle) cast   **106**
Samples, Geoff   63, 68, 99, 103, 116
Seniors   **37-41**
Shooting line   24, 27, 35, 44, **75-78**, 81, 82, 100, 102, 110, 111, 116, 122
Sidearm cast   **70-71**, 101, 106
Single haul   67, 79, 82, 87, 88, 91, **94-95**
Sinking line   34, 38, 83, **85-93**
Sinking-tip line   **85-88**, 94, 113
Slack   39, **58-60**, 96, 105, 106
Snake ("S," wiggle) cast   **106**
Speed cast   **110-112**
Stance   64
Stidham, Mike   6
Strength exercises   **42-44**
Stripping basket   112
Swisher, Doug   26, 106, 121
Swisher, Randi   26, 69
Tailing loops   68, **72-74**, 123
Tape measure   77, 80, 97

Thumb and forefinger (combination) grip   48
Thumb/thumb-on-top grip   47
Tight loops   23, 24, 26, 38, 56, 57, 68, 69, **70,** 71, 73, 75, 80, 88, 90, 91, 92, 94, 100
Trout Unlimited   6
Tuck cast   106-107
Underpowering   66, 73, 106
"V" grip   47
Video   54, 96, 103, 118, **121**
Wiggle ("S," snake) cast   **106**
Wind   21, 57, 60, 68, 72, 74, 79, 80, 90. 94, 95, 96, **99-102**
Woods, Tiger   51, 120, 124
Wulff, Joan   6, 36, 48, 118
Women   **33-36,** 52, 116
Wind   19-21, 38, 43, 48, **55-57,** 65, 70, 73, 90, 91. 100
Youth   **28-32,** 63, 78, 103, 118

AMAZINGOUTDOORS.COM RESOURCES

AmazingOutdoors.com AmazingOutdoors.com is the premier outdoors-related web site for recreation and information in the Intermountain West. The site features multimedia presentations, maps, magazine content from the past 13 years of *Utah Outdoors* magazine (an AmazingOutdoors.com subsidiary, formerly *Utah Fishing and Outdoors*), and news and feature stories dedicated to all forms of outdoor recreation. This content-intensive site also includes the complete contents of many guidebooks from Falcon Publishing, those from AmazingOutdoors.com and its other subsidiaries, and updated weather and fishing reports, including our weekly FishBytes e-mail, as well as an online retail shop where users can purchase hundreds of items. Phone numbers for more information on AO.com and its affiliates, or to order any of the publications below (also available at bookstores and sporting goods stores): (801) 858-3450 or toll-free (800) 366-8824.

Rocky Mountain Fly Fishing Provides detailed information on regulations, tactics, fish species, best season to go and more on blue ribbon rivers throughout the West, as well as sections on whirling disease, wading safety, using GPS and choosing watercraft.

Utah Fishing Guide The most comprehensive guide ever published on fishing in Utah. Regulations and fishing tips for over 700 waters. GPS coordinates, maps, techniques and description of facilities. Extensive sections cover the Uinta and Boulder Mountain areas.

Utah Boating Guide A comprehensive guide to all boatable waters in Utah. Provides maps and photos for all waters, along with descriptions of the waters, facilities, unique features and suggested activities. Also includes sections on boating skills, safety and regulations. Published by UtahOutdoors.com; available per above and at boat dealerships.

Utah Camping Guide A comprehensive guide to public and private campgrounds in Utah and significant over-the-border destinations, including Grand Canyon and Yellowstone national parks, grouped by region. Provides directions to campgrounds and describes facilities. Also provides basic information on planning campouts and on camping skills.

Utah Outdoors **magazine** A monthly magazine describing the Intermountain West's best fishing, hiking, backpacking, mountain biking and exploring adventures. In-depth coverage of fishing on quality waters from the Yellowstone area through southern Idaho, all of Utah, and south to Wahweap and Lees Ferry in Arizona. Also covers family adventures and destinations. Mailed to subscribers and sold over the counter at stores throughout the region.

FishBytes A free, weekly e-mail newsletter published by Utah Outdoors. FishBytes is mailed every Thursday evening and is designed to help anglers plan weekend fishing adventures. It contains the latest information possible on the best places to fish in the Intermountain Region, including information on hatches and fly patterns. To subscribe, follow the links on www.AmazingOutdoors.com.

Utah Trout Map A 3D-relief map of Utah identifying trout waters. Color codes show the waters quality rating, making it eaasy to locate the best fishing in the state. This is a beautiful work suitable for framing and display as an art piece. It is also available as a fold-up map — throw it into the glove compartment and use it for field reference.

Provo River Map and Fishing Guide Shows access points, prominent holes and features, and describes effective fishing techniques.

About the author

Berris "Bear" Samples is a master certified casting instructor with over five years experience teaching in affiliation with Sage Rod Company. He has fished around the world, including most of Europe, Canada, Mexico, the U.S. and Christmas Island.

In 1991 Samples received the Federation of Fly Fishers' Ambassador of the Year award for promoting international conservation and good will. He has written flyfishing articles for magazines in America and Europe, and is a lifetime member of the Federation of Fly Fishers and Trout Unlimited. Samples is pastor of Park City Community Church in Utah and has served 27 years of duty as an Army Reserve chaplain.

NOTES

UTAH OUTDOORS
M A G A Z I N E

For the price of a night at the movies for two, you'll learn about the best places in Utah and surrounding areas to boat, fish, hike, camp, mountain bike and explore — every month, all year long. It's our job to know about the hot new destinations, the old favorites and the overlooked places — and to tell you all about them, with stories, maps and photos. We'll keep you informed, up-to-date and ahead of the crowds.

To start your subscription, just fill out the information on this card and mail it in. We'll bill you later.

For questions or credit card service, call 1(800) 366-UTAH.

Name _____ Phone _____

Address _____

City _____ State _____ Zip _____

E-mail address _____

12 issues for $19.95*

*plus tax

Also...

If you're an outdoor enthusiast, you'll likely be interested in our other products and publications:

- ❏ **Bear's Casting Aid,** by Bear Samples, $5.95*
  A comfortable strap that teaches casters to hold their wrists and rods in proper position

- ❏ **Rocky Mountain Flyfishing,** by Steve Cook, $24.95*
  Fly patterns, hatch charts, regulations, tips, maps, GPS coordinates and more — 416 pages, softbound

- ❏ **Utah Camping Guide,** by Gaylen Webb, $19.95*
  Directions, descriptions, fees & reservations, tips and more — 240 pages, softbound

- ❏ **Utah Trout map,** $5.95*
  Ranks waters according to quality of fishing — 24"x32", two-sided, suitable for framing

- ❏ **Provo River map,** $5.95*
  Fishing the Provo River drainage and related waters — 24"x32", two-sided

*Plus tax and shipping

Send no money now. Just return this card with your selections marked and we will bill you. For faster service, call 1 (800) 366-UTAH or visit us on the web at www.AmazingOutdoors.com.

Name _____ Phone _____

Address _____

City _____ State _____ Zip _____

E-mail address _____

Amazing Outdoors.com

PLACE STAMP HERE

UtahOutdoors

P.O. Box 711126
Salt Lake City, UT 84171-1126

PLACE STAMP HERE

AmazingOutdoors.com

P.O. Box 711126
Salt Lake City, UT 84171-1126